A CRITIQUE OF ANARCHIST COMMUNISM

Publisher's note on style:
There have been no changes to the text itself besides formatting changes. I have retained the British spelling of words, any references the text makes should be read in the context that it was written for, as described in the Foreword.
There are two types of notes presented to the reader. A footnote, found at the bottom of the page, is designated in the text by a superscript asterisk (*), whereas an endnote is demarcated by a superscript number ([9]). All endnotes are found in the back of the book.

Many thanks to
SVEIN OLAV NYBERG, TREVOR BLAKE

Designed and edited by
KEVIN I. SLAUGHTER

Published by
UNDERWORLD AMUSEMENTS
ISBN: 978-1943687060

STAND ALONE
SA1030

More information at:
WWW.UNIONOFEGOISTS.COM
WWW.UNDERWORLDAMUSEMENTS.COM

FOREWORD

The world has changed a great deal since I wrote "A CRITIQUE OF ANARCHIST COMMUNISM" back in 1971, but my views on the subject have changed very little. Apart from a few things, like the disastrous effect of the gold standard on working men and women, I see little in my original essay which I would change substantially.*

Forty-five years ago I was asked by Bill Dwyer, the editor of the English monthly journal *Anarchy*, to write an article critiquing anarchist-communism and offering an individualist-anarchist alternative to it, but just before its scheduled appearance as issue #119 the magazine folded. I then sent the manuscript to the American quarterly *Libertarian Analysis* and just before it was scheduled to appear in its fifth issue in 1972, it too suffered the same fate as its overseas sister publication. Then, in 1983, Carl Watner published the chapter "Revolution: The Road to Freedom?" in issue #6 of his bimonthly, *The Voluntaryist*. Eventually, in 1992 Svein Olav Nyberg agreed to run the entire article as a serial in his newly established online periodical, *Non Serviam*. Finally, during the summer of 2009, Wendy McElroy posted the whole essay in six parts on her anarchist-feminist blog, WendyMcElroy.com.

Now, at last, Kevin I. Slaughter has proposed putting my magnum opus between the covers of an actual book! I am grateful to The Union of Egoists' *Stand Alone* project for taking on the task of publishing this essay from a time which

---

* Nixon, unilaterally cancelling the international convertibility of the U.S. dollar to gold a few months after my essay was written, effectively rendered the Bretton Woods system inoperative and decoupled the world economy from gold—replacing it with something even worse, i.e. money based on government fiat

differs in many ways from our own. The section on communism may seem antiquated after the fall of the Soviet empire, as well as the economic analysis focusing on the capitalists' monopoly of a limited money supply in the form of gold, but the section which should be of most interest to readers drawn to The Union of Egoists will be the one on Max Stirner's egoism, which is timeless.

KEN KNUDSON
menckenfan@gmail.com
Annecy-le-Vieux, France
October, 2016

A Critique of ANARCHIST COMMUNISM

by Ken Knudson

A NOTE TO READERS

I address myself in these pages primarily to those readers of *Anarchy* who call themselves "communist-anarchists." It is my purpose in this article to show that this label is a contradiction in terms and that anyone accepting it must do so by a lack of clear understanding of what the words "anarchist" and "communist" really mean. It is my hope that in driving a wedge between these two words, the communist side will suffer at the expense of the anarchist.

I make no claims to originality in these pages. Most of what I have to say has been said before and much better. The economics is taken primarily from the writings of Pierre-Joseph Proudhon, William B. Greene, and Benjamin R. Tucker. The philosophy from Max Stirner, Tucker again, and, to a lesser extent, James L. Walker.

I hope you won't be put off by my clumsy prose. I'm a scientist by trade, not a professional writer. I implore you, therefore, not to mistake style for content. If you want both the content and good style may I suggest Tucker's "Instead of a Book". Unfortunately, this volume has been out of print since 1897, but the better libraries—especially those in the United States—should have it. If you can read French, I recommend the economic writings of Proudhon. *General Idea of the Revolution in the Nineteenth Century* is particularly good and has been translated into English by the American individualist, John Beverley Robinson. (Freedom Press, 1923). Also in English is Tucker's translation of one of Proudhon's earliest works, the well-known *What is Property?*. This book is not as good as the *General Idea* book, but it has the advantage of being currently available in paperback in both languages. A word of warning: unless you are thoroughly familiar with

Proudhon, I would not recommend the popular Macmillan "Papermac" edition of *Selected Writings of Pierre-Joseph Proudhon*; they seem to have been selected with irrelevance as their only criterion. Like so many other great writers, Proudhon suffers tremendously when quoted out of context and this particular edition gives, on average, less than a page per selection. Better to read his worst book completely than to be misled by disconnected excerpts like these. Finally the individualist philosophy, egoism, is best found in Max Stirner's *The Ego and His Own*. This book suffers somewhat from a very difficult style (which wasn't aided by Stirner's wariness of the Prussian censor), but if you can get through his obscure references and biblical quotes, I think you will find the task worth the effort.

H. L. Mencken once observed that just because a rose smells better than a cabbage doesn't mean to say it makes a better soup. I feel the same way about individualist anarchism. At first whiff, the altruist rose may smell better than the individualist cabbage, but the former sure makes a lousy soup. In the following pages I hope to show that the latter makes a better one.

KEN KNUDSON
Geneva, Switzerland
March, 1971

COMMUNISM: FOR THE COMMON GOOD

"Communism is a 9 letter word used by inferior magicians with the wrong alchemical formula for transforming earth into gold."
—ALLEN GINSBERG, *Wichita Vortex Sutra*

By way of prelude to the individualist critique of communism, I should like to look briefly at the communist-anarchists' critique of their Marxist brothers. Anarchists and Marxists have traditionally been at odds with one another: Bakunin and Marx split the First International over their differences a century ago; Emma Goldman virtually made her living in the 1920's from writing books and magazine articles about her "disillusionment in Russia"; in May, 1937, the communists and anarchists took time off from their war against Franco to butcher each other in the streets of Barcelona; and the May days of '68 saw French anarchists directing more abuse against the communist CGT than against the Gaullist government.

What is the nature of these differences? Perhaps the most concise answer to this question came in 1906 from a veritable expert on the subject: Joseph Stalin. He wrote in *Anarchism or Socialism?* that there were essentially three main accusations which (communist) anarchists leveled against Marxism:

1) that the Marxists aren't really communists because they would "preserve the two institutions which constitute the foundation of [the capitalist] system: representative government and wage labour";[1]

2) that the Marxists "are not revolutionaries", "repudiate violent revolution", and "want to establish Socialism only by means of ballot papers";[2]

3) that the Marxists "actually want to establish not the dictatorship of the proletariat, but their own dictatorship over

the proletariat."[3] Stalin goes on to quote Marx and Engels to "prove" that "everything the anarchists say on this subject is either the result of stupidity, or despicable slander."[4] Today the anarchists have the advantage of history on their side to show just who was slandering whom. I won't insult the reader's intelligence by pointing out how all three objections to Marxism were sustained by Uncle Joe himself a few decades later.

But let us look at these three accusations from another point of view. Aren't the communist-anarchists simply saying in their holier-than-thou attitude, "I'm more communist than you, I'm more revolutionary than you, I'm more consistent than you?" What's wrong with Marxism, they say, is NOT that it is for communism, violent revolution and dictatorship, but that it goes about attaining its goals by half-measures, compromises, and pussyfooting around. Individualist-anarchists have a different criticism. We reject communism per se, violent revolution per se, and dictatorship per se. My purpose here is to try to explain why.

Before one can get into an intelligent criticism of anything, one must begin by defining one's terms. "Anarchism", according to the *Encyclopaedia Britannica* dictionary, is "the theory that all forms of government are incompatible with individual and social liberty and should be abolished." It further says that it comes from the Greek roots "an" (without) and "archos" (leader).* As for "communism", it is "any social theory that calls for the abolition of private property and control by the community over economic affairs." To elaborate on that definition, communists of all varieties hold that all wealth should be produced and distributed according to the formula "from each according to his** ability, to each according to

---

*   Historically, it was Proudhon who first used the word to mean something other than disorder and chaos: "Although a firm friend of order, I am (in the full force of the term) an anarchist."[5]

**   Here Marx uses the masculine pronoun to denote the generic "one". In deference to easy flowing English grammar, I'll stick to his precedent and

his needs" and that the administrative mechanism to control such production and distribution should be democratically organised by the workers themselves (i.e. "workers' control"). They further insist that there should be no private ownership of the means of production and no trading of goods except through the official channels agreed upon by the majority. With rare exceptions, communists of all varieties propose to realise this ideal through violent revolution and the expropriation of all private property.

That no one should accuse me of building up straw men in order to knock them down, allow me to quote Kropotkin* to show that communist-anarchism fits in well with the above definition of communism:

"We have to put an end to the iniquities, the vices, the crimes which result from the idle existence of some and the economic, intellectual, and moral servitude of others.... We are no longer obliged to grope in the dark for the solution.... It is Expropriation.... If all accumulated treasure...does not immediately go back to the collectivity—since ALL have contributed to produce it; if the insurgent people do not take possession of all the goods and provisions amassed in the great cities and do not organise to put them within the reach of all who need them...the insurrection will not be a revolution, and everything will have to be begun over again.... Expropriation,—that then, is the watchword which is imposed upon the next revolution, under penalty of failing in its historic mission. The complete expropriation of all who have the means of exploiting human beings. The return to common ownership by the nation of all that can serve in the

---

hope that Women's Lib people will forgive me when I, too, write "his" instead of "one's".

*   I have chosen Kropotkin as a "typical" communist-anarchist here and elsewhere in this article for a number of reasons. First, he was a particularly prolific writer, doing much of his original work in English. Secondly, he is generally regarded as "probably the greatest anarchist thinker and writer" by many communist-anarchists, including at least one editor of *Freedom*.[6] Finally, he was the founder of Freedom Press, the publisher of the magazine this essay was originally written for.

hands of any one for the exploitation of others."[7]

Now let us take our definitions of communism and anarchism and see where they lead us. The first part of the definition of communism calls for the abolition of private property. "Abolition" is itself a rather authoritarian concept—unless, of course, you're talking about abolishing something which is inherently authoritarian and invasive itself (like slavery or government, for example). So the question boils down to "Is private property authoritarian and invasive?" The communists answer "yes"; the individualists disagree. Who is right? Which is the more "anarchistic" answer? The communists argue that "private property has become a hindrance to the evolution of mankind towards happiness"[8], that "private property offends against justice"[9] and that it "has developed parasitically amidst the free institutions of our earliest ancestors."[10] The individualists, far from denying these assertions, reaffirm them. After all wasn't it Proudhon who first declared property "theft"?* But when the communist says, "Be done, then, with this vile institution; abolish private property once and for all; expropriate and collectivise all property for the common good," the individualist must part company with him. What's wrong with private property today is that it rests primarily in the hands of a legally privileged elite. The resolution of this injustice is not to perpetrate an even greater one, but rather to devise a social and economic system which will distribute property in such a manner that everyone is guaranteed the product of his labour by natural economic laws. I propose to demonstrate just such a system at the end of this article. If this can be done, it will have been shown that private property is not intrinsically invasive after all, and that the communists in expropriating it would be committing a most UNanarchistic act. It is, therefore, incumbent upon all communists who call themselves anarchists to read carefully

---

* By property Proudhon means property as it exists under government privilege, i.e. property gained not through labour or the exchange of the products of labour (which he favours), but through the legal privileges bestowed by government on idle capital.

that section and either find a flaw in its reasoning or admit that they are not anarchists after all.

The second part of the definition of communism says that economic affairs should be controlled by the community. Individualists say they should be controlled by the market place and that the only law should be the natural law of supply and demand. Which of these two propositions is the more consistent with anarchism? Herbert Spencer wrote in 1884, "The great political superstition of the past was the divine right of kings. The great political superstition of the present is the divine right of parliaments."[11] The communists seem to have carried Spencer's observation one step further: the great political superstition of the future shall be the divine right of workers' majorities. "Workers' control" is their ideology; "Power to the People" their battle cry. What communist-anarchists apparently forget is that workers' control means CONTROL. Marxists, let it be said to their credit, at least are honest about this point. They openly and unashamedly demand the dictatorship of the proletariat. Communist-anarchists seem to be afraid of that phrase, perhaps subconsciously realising the inherent contradiction in their position. But communism, by its very nature, IS dictatorial. The communist-anarchists may christen their governing bodies "workers' councils" or "soviets", but they remain GOVERNMENTS just the same.

Abraham Lincoln was supposed to have asked, "If you call a tail a leg, how many legs has a dog? Five? No! Calling a tail a leg don't MAKE it a leg." The same is true about governments and laws. Calling a law a "social habit"[12] or an "unwritten custom"[13] as Kropotkin does, doesn't change its nature. To paraphrase Shakespeare, that which we call a law by any other name would smell as foul.

Let us take a closer look at the type of society the communists would have us live under and see if we can get at the essence of these laws. Kropotkin says that "nine-tenths of those called lazy...are people gone astray."[14] He then suggests that given a job which "answers" their "temperament" and "capacities" (today we would hear words like "relate", "alienation" and "relevancy"), these people would be productive workers for the community. What about that other ten percent which couldn't adjust? Kropotkin doesn't elaborate, but he does say, "if not one, of the thousands of groups of our federation, will receive you, whatever be their motive; if you are absolutely incapable of producing anything useful, or if you refuse to do it, then live like an isolated man....That is what could be done in a communal society in order to turn away sluggards if they become too numerous."[15] This is a pretty harsh sentence considering that ALL the means of production have been confiscated in the name of the revolution. So we see that communism's law, put bluntly, becomes "work or starve."* This happens to be an individualist law too. But there is a difference between the two: the communist law is a man-made law, subject to man's emotions, rationalisations, and inconsistencies; the individualist law is nature's law—the law of gastric juices, if you will—a law which, like it or not, is beyond repeal. Although both laws use the same language, the difference in meaning is the difference between a commandment and a scientific observation. Individualist-anarchists don't care when, where, or how a man earns a living, as long as he is not invasive about it. He may work 18 hours a day and buy a mansion to live in the other six hours if he so chooses. Or he may feel like Thoreau did that "that man is richest whose pleasures are the cheapest"[16] and work but a few hours a week to ensure his livelihood. I wonder what would happen to Thoreau under communism? Kropotkin would undoubtedly look upon him as "a ghost of bourgeois society."[17] And what would Thoreau say to Kropotkin's proposed "contract"?: "We undertake to give you the use of our houses, stores, streets, means of transport, schools, museums, etc., on condition that, from twenty to forty-five or fifty years

_____

*   Article 12 of the 1936 constitution of the USSR reads: "In the USSR work is the duty of every able-bodied citizen according to the principle: 'He who does not work, neither shall he eat.' In the USSR the principle of socialism is realised: 'From each according to his ability, to each according to his work.'"

of age, you consecrate four or five hours a day to some work recognised [by whom?] as necessary to existence....Twelve or fifteen hundred hours of work a year...is all we ask of you."[18] I don't think it would be pulling the nose of reason to argue that Thoreau would object to these terms.

But some communist-anarchists would reject Kropotkin's idea of not giving to the unproductive worker according to his needs, even if he doesn't contribute according to his abilities. They might simply say that Kropotkin wasn't being a good communist when he wrote those lines (just as he wasn't being a good anarchist when he supported the Allies during World War I). But this idea, it seems to me would be patently unjust to the poor workers who would have to support such parasites. How do these communists reconcile such an injustice? As best I can gather from the writings of the classical communist-anarchists, they meet this problem in one of two ways: (1) they ignore it, or (2) they deny it. Malatesta takes the first approach. When asked, "How will production and distribution be organised?" he replies that anarchists are not prophets and that they have no blueprints for the future. Indeed, he likens this important question to asking when a man "should go to bed and on what days he should cut his nails."[19] Alexander Berkman takes the other approach (a notion apparently borrowed from the Marxists*): he denies that unproductive men will exist after the revolution. "In an anarchist society it will be the most useful and difficult toil that one will seek rather than the lighter job."[20] Berkman's view of labour makes the protestant work ethic sound positively mild by comparison. For example: "Can you doubt that even the hardest toil would become a pleasure...in an atmosphere of brotherhood and respect for labour?"[21] Yes, I can doubt it. Or again: "We can visualise the time when labour will have become a pleasant exercise, a joyous application of physical effort to the needs of the world."[22] And again, in apparent

---

* At least Berkman is consistent in this matter. Marx, paradoxically, wanted to both "abolish labour itself" (*The German Ideology*), AND make it "life's prime want" (*Critique of the Gotha Programme*).

anticipation of Goebbles' famous dictum about the powers of repetition, "Work will become a pleasure... laziness will be unknown."[23] It is hard to argue with such "reasoning". It would be like a debate between Bertrand Russell and Billy Graham about the existence of heaven. How can you argue with faith? I won't even try. I'll just ask the reader, next time he is at work, to look around—at himself and at his mates—and ask himself this question: "After the revolution will we really prefer this place to staying at home in bed or going off to the seashore?" If there are enough people who can an-swer "yes" to this question perhaps communism will work after all. But in the meantime, before building the barricades and shooting people for a cause of dubious certainty, I would suggest pondering these two items from the bourgeois and communist press respectively:

> "In Detroit's auto plants, weekend absenteeism has reached such proportions that a current bit of folk wis-dom advises car buyers to steer clear of vehicles made on a Monday or Friday. Inexperienced substitute workers, so the caution goes, have a way of building bugs into a car. But in Italy lately the warning might well include Tuesday, Wednesday, and Thursday. At Fiat, the coun-try's largest maker, absenteeism has jumped this year from the normal 4 or 5 percent to 12.5 percent, with as many as 18,000 workers failing to clock in for daily shifts at the company's Turin works. Alfa Romeo's rate has hit 15 percent as hundreds of workers call in each day with 'malattia di comodo'—a convenient illness.... Italian auto workers seem to be doing no more than taking advantage of a very good deal. A new labour contract guarantees workers in state-controlled industries 180 days of sick leave a year, at full pay, while workers in private firms (such as Fiat) get the same number of days at 75 percent of full pay."[24]

When doctors, employed by the state, made an inspection

visit in Turin we are told that they found "that only 20 percent of the 'indisposed' workers they had visited were even mildly sick." For those who think that this is just a bourgeois aberration, let us see what revolutionary Cuba, after 12 years of communism, has to say about such "parasites". I translate from the official organ of the Central Committee of the Cuban Communist Party:

"Worker's discussion groups are being set up in all work centres to discuss the proposed law against laziness. These groups have already proven to be a valuable forum for the working class. During these assemblies, which for the moment are limited to pilot projects in the Havana area, workers have made original suggestions and posed timely questions which lead one to believe that massive discussion of this type would make a notable contribution to the solution of this serious problem. An assembly of boiler repairmen in the Luyano district was representative of the general feeling of the workers. They demanded that action be taken against those parasitic students who have stopped going to classes regularly or who, although attending classes, do just enough to get by. The workers were equally adamant about co-workers who, after a sickness or accident, refuse to go back to their jobs but go on receiving their salaries for months without working. Questions were often accompanied by concrete proposals. For example, should criminals receive the same salaries on coming back to work from prison as when they left their jobs? The workers thought not, but they did think it all right that the revolutionary state accord a pension to the prisoner's family during his stay in the re-education [sic] centre. At the Papelera Cubana factory the workers made a suggestion which proved their contempt of these loafers; habitual offenders should be punished in geometric proportion to the number of their crimes. They also proposed that workers who quit their jobs or were absent too often be condemned to a minimum, not of 6 months, but of one year's imprisonment and that the worker who refuses three times work proposed by the Ministry of Labour be considered automatically as a criminal and subject to punishment as such. The workers also expressed doubts about the scholastic 'deserters', ages 15 and 16, who aren't yet considered physically and mentally able to work but who don't study either. They also cited the case of the self employed man who works only for his own selfish interests. The dockworkers of Havana port, zone 1, also had their meeting. They envisioned the possibility of making this law retroactive for those who have a bad work attitude, stating forcefully that it wasn't a question of precedents, because otherwise the law could only be applied in those cases which occurred after its enactment. The harbour workers also proposed imprisonment for the 'sanctioned' workers and that, in their opinion, the punishment of these parasites shouldn't be lifted until they could demonstrate a change of attitude. The steadfastness of the workers was clearly demonstrated when they demanded that punishments not be decided by the workers themselves in order to avoid possible leniency due to reasons of sympathy, sentimentality, etc. The workers also indicated that these parasites should not have the right to the social benefits accorded to other workers. Some workers considered imprisonment as a measure much too kind. As you can see, the workers have made many good proposals, which leads us to believe that with massive discussion, this new law will be considerably enriched. This is perhaps the path to social legislation by the masses.'"[25]

----

*   The Associated Press has since reported the passage of this law: "Cuba's Communist regime announced yesterday a tough new labour law that Premier Fidel Castro said is aimed at 400,000 loafers, bums and 'parasites' who have upset the country's new social order. The law, which goes into effect April 1, provides for penalties ranging from six months to two years of forced labour in 'rehabilitation centres' for those convicted of vagrancy, malingering or habitual absenteeism from work or school. The law decrees that all males between 17 and 60 have a 'social duty' to work on a daily systematic basis unless they

These two extracts clearly demonstrate that human nature remains pretty constant, independent of the social system the individual workman is subjected to. So it seems to me that unless human nature can somehow be miraculously transformed by the revolution—and that WOULD be a revolution—some form of compulsion would be necessary in order to obtain "from each according to his abilities."

While on this point, I would like to ask my communist-anarchist comrades just who is supposed to determine another person's abilities? We've seen from the above article that in Cuba the Ministry of Labour makes this decision. How would it differ in an anarchist commune? If these anarchists are at all consistent with their professed desire for individual freedom, the only answer to this question is that the individual himself would be the sole judge of his abilities and, hence, his profession. But this is ridiculous. Who, I wonder, is going to decide of his own free will that his real ability lies in collecting other people's garbage? And what about the man who thinks that he is the greatest artist since Leonardo da Vinci and decides to devote his life to painting mediocre landscapes while the community literally feeds his delusions with food from the communal warehouse? Few people, I dare say, would opt to do the necessary "dirty work" if they could choose with impunity ANY job, knowing that whatever they did—good or bad, hard or easy—they would still receive according to their needs.* The individualist's answer

---

are attending an approved school. Those who do not are considered 'parasites of the revolution' and subject to prosecution by the courts or special labourers' councils. The anti-loafing law—seen as a tough new weapon to be used mainly against dissatisfied young people—was prompted by Mr. Castro's disclosure last September that as many as 400,000 workers were creating serious economic problems by shirking their duties."[26]

*   Anyone who has ever gone to an anarchist summer camp knows what I mean. Here we have "la creme de la creme", so to speak, just dying to get on with the revolution; yet who cleans out the latrines? More often than not, no one. Or, when it really gets bad, some poor sap will sacrifice himself for the cause. You don't have solidarity; you have martyrdom. And no one feels good about it: you have resentment on the part of the guy who does it and guilt from those who don't.

to this perennial question of "who will do the dirty work" is very simple: "I will if I'm paid well enough." I suspect even Mr. Heath would go down into the London sewers if he were paid 5 million pounds per hour for doing it. Somewhere between this sum and what a sewer worker now gets is a just wage, which, given a truly free society, would be readily determined by competition. This brings us to the second half of the communist ideal: the distribution of goods according to need. The obvious question again arises, "Who is to decide what another man needs?" Anarchists once more must leave that decision up to the individual involved. To do otherwise would be to invite tyranny, for who can better determine a person's needs than the person himself?* But if the individual is to decide for himself what he needs, what is to prevent him from "needing" a yacht and his own private airplane? If you think we've got a consumer society now, what would it be like if everything was free for the needing? You may object that luxuries aren't needs. But that is just begging the question: what is a luxury, after all? To millions of people in the world today food is a luxury. To the English central heating is a luxury, while to the Americans it's a necessity. The Nazi concentration camps painfully demonstrated just how little man actually NEEDS. But is that the criterion communists would use for determining need? I should hope (and think) not. So it seems to me that this posses a definite dilemma for the communist-anarchist: what do you do about unreasonable, irrational, or extravagant "needs"? What about the man who "needs" a new pair of shoes every month? "Nonsense," you may say, "no one needs new shoes that often." Well, how often then? Once a year? Every five years perhaps? And who will decide? Then what about me? I live in Switzerland and I'm crazy about grape jam—but unfortunately the Swiss aren't. I feel that a jam sandwich isn't a jam sandwich unless it's

---

* I'm reminded here of the tale of the man who decided his mule didn't NEED any food. He set out to demonstrate his theory and almost proved his point when, unfortunately, the beast died. Authoritarian communism runs a similar risk when it attempts to determine the needs of others.

made with GRAPE jam. But tell that to the Swiss! If Switzerland were a communist federation, there wouldn't be a single communal warehouse which would stock grape jam. If I were to go up to the commissar-in-charge-of-jams and ask him to put in a requisition for a few cases, he would think I was nuts. "Grapes are for wine," he'd tell me with infallible logic, "and more people drink wine than eat grape jam." "But I'm a vegetarian," I plead, "and just think of all the money (?) I'm saving the commune by not eating any of that expensive meat." After which he would lecture me on the economics of jam making, tell me that a grape is more valuable in its liquid form, and chastise me for being a throwback to bourgeois decadence.

And what about you, dear reader? Have you no individual idiosyncrasies? Perhaps you've got a thing about marshmallows. What if the workers in the marshmallow factories decide (under workers' control, of course) that marshmallows are bad for your health, too difficult to make, or just simply a capitalist plot? Are you to be denied the culinary delights that only marshmallows can offer, simply because some distant workers get it into their heads that a marshmallowless world would be a better world?

But, not only would distribution according to need hurt the consumer, it would be grossly unfair to the productive worker who actually makes the goods or performs the necessary services. Suppose, for example, that hardworking farmer Brown goes to the communal warehouse with a load of freshly dug potatoes. While there Brown decides he needs a new pair of boots. Unfortunately there are only a few pairs in stock since Jones the shoemaker quit his job—preferring to spend his days living off Brown's potatoes and writing sonnets about the good life. So boots are rationed. The boot commissar agrees that Brown's boots are pretty shabby but, he points out, Smith the astrologer is in even greater need. Could Brown come back in a month or so when BOTH soles have worn through? Brown walks away in disgust, resolved never again to sweat over his potato patch.

Even today people are beginning to complain about the

injustices of the (relatively mild) welfare state. Theodore Roszak writes that in British schools there has been a "strong trend away from the sciences over the past four years" and that people are showing "annoyed concern" and "loudly observing that the country is not spending its money to produce poets and Egyptologists—and then demanding a sharp cut in university grants and stipends."[27] If people are upset NOW at the number of poets and Egyptologists that they are supporting, what would it be like if EVERYONE could simply take up his favourite hobby as his chosen profession? I suspect it wouldn't be long before our professional chess players and mountain climbers found the warehouse stocks dwindling to nothing. Social unrest would surely increase in direct proportion to the height of the trash piling up on the doorsteps and the subsequent yearning for the "good old days" would bring about the inevitable counter-revolution. Such would be the fate of the anarchist-communist utopia.

Peter Kropotkin opens his chapter on "Consumption and Production" in *The Conquest of Bread* with the following words:

> "If you open the works of any economist you will find that he begins with PRODUCTION, the analysis of means employed nowadays for the creation of wealth; division of labour, manufacture, machinery, accumulation of capital. From Adam Smith to Marx, all have proceeded along these lines. Only in the latter parts of their books do they treat of CONSUMPTION, that is to say, of the means necessary to satisfy the needs of individuals....Perhaps you will say this is logical. Before satisfying needs you must create the wherewithal to satisfy them. But before producing anything, must you not feel the need of it? Is it not necessity that first drove man to hunt, to raise cattle, to cultivate land, to make implements, and later on to invent machinery? Is it not the study of needs that should govern production?"[28]

When I first came upon these words, I must admit I was rather surprised. "What have we here," I thought, "is the prince of anarchist-communism actually going to come out in favour of the consumer?" It didn't take long to find out that he wasn't. Most communists try very hard to ignore the fact that the sole purpose of production is consumption. But not Kropotkin; he first recognises the fact—and THEN he ignores it. It's only a matter of three pages before he gets his head back into the sand and talks of "how to reorganise PRODUCTION so as to really satisfy all needs."*

Under communism it is not the consumer that counts; it is the producer. The consumer is looked upon with scorn—a loathsome, if necessary, evil. The worker, on the other hand, is depicted as all that is good and heroic. It is not by accident that the hammer and sickle find themselves as the symbols of the Russian "workers' paradise." Can you honestly imagine a communist society raising the banner of bread and butter and declaring the advent of the "consumers' paradise"? If you can, your imagination is much more vivid than mine.

But that's exactly what individualist-anarchists would do. Instead of the communist's "workers' control" (i.e. a producers' democracy), we advocate a consumers' democracy. Both democracies—like all democracies—would in fact be dictatorships. The question for anarchists is which dictatorship is the least oppressive? The answer should be obvious. But, judging from the ratio of communists to individualists in the anarchist movement, apparently it's not. So perhaps I'd better explain.

The workers in some given industry decide that item A should no longer be produced and decide instead to manufacture item B. Now consumer X, who never liked item A anyway, couldn't care less; but poor Y feels his life will never be the same without A. What can Y do? He's just a lone consumer and consumers have no rights in this society. But maybe other Y's agree with him. A survey is taken and it is

---

*   Emphasis added.

shown that only 3% of all consumers regret the passing of A. But can't some compromise be arrived at? How about letting just one tiny factory make A's? Perhaps the workers agree to this accommodation. Perhaps not. In any case the workers' decision is final. There is no appeal. The Y's are totally at the mercy of the workers and if the decision is adverse, they'll just have to swallow hard and hope that next week item C isn't taken away as well. So much for the producers' dictatorship.

Let's now take a look at the consumers' dictatorship. Consumers are finicky people—they want the best possible product at the lowest possible price. To achieve this end they will use ruthless means. The fact that producer X asks more for his product than Y asks for his similar product is all that the consumer needs to know. He will mercilessly buy Y's over X's. The extenuating circumstances matter little to him. X may have ten children and a mother-in-law to feed. The consumer still buys from Y. Such is the nature of the consumers' dictatorship over the producer.

Now there is a fundamental difference between these two dictatorships. In the one the worker says to the consumer, "I will produce what I want and if you don't like it you can lump it." In the other the consumer says to the worker, "You will produce what I want and if you don't I will take my business elsewhere." It doesn't take the sensitive antennae of an anarchist to see which of these two statements is the more authoritarian. The first leaves no room for argument; there are no exceptions, no loopholes for the dissident consumer to crawl through. The second, on the other hand, leaves a loophole so big that it is limited only by the worker's imagination and abilities. If a producer is not doing as well as his competitor, there's a reason for it. He may not be suited for that particular work, in which case he will change jobs. He may be charging too much for his goods or services, in which case he will have to lower his costs, profits, and/or overhead to meet the competition. But one thing should be made clear: each worker is also a consumer and what the individual looses in his role as producer by having to cut his costs down to the competitive market level, he makes up in his role as consumer by being able to buy at the lowest possible prices.*

Let us turn our attention now to the various philosophies used by communists to justify their social system. The exponents of any social change invariably claim that people will be "happier" under their system than they now are under the status quo. The big metaphysical question then becomes, "What is happiness?" Up until recently the communists—materialists par excellence—used to say it was material well-being. The main gripe they had against capitalism was that the workers were NECESSARILY in a state of increasing poverty. Bakunin, echoing Marx, said that "the situation of the proletariat...by virtue of inevitable economic law, must and will become worse every year."[29] But since World War II this pillar of communist thought has become increasingly shaky—particularly in the United States where "hard hats" are now pulling in salaries upwards of four quid an hour. This fact has created such acute embarrassment among the faithful that many communists are now seeking a new definition of happiness which has nothing to do with material comfort.

Very often what they do in discarding the Marxist happiness albatross is to saddle themselves with a Freudian one.** The new definition of happiness our neo-Freudian communists arrive at is usually derived from what Otto Fenichel called the "Nirvana principle." The essence of this theory is that both life-enhancing behaviour (e.g. sexual intercourse,

* The usual objection raised to a "consumers' democracy" is that capitalists have used similar catch phrases in order to justify capitalism and keep the workers in a subjugated position. Individualists sustain this objection but point out that capitalists are being inconsistent by not practicing what they preach. If they did, they would no longer be in a position of privilege, living off the labour of others. This point is made clear in the section on capitalism later in this article.

** Wilhelm Reich and R. D. Laing are among the latest gurus of the libertarian left. And it's not uncommon in anarchist circles to hear a few sympathetic words about Herbert Marcuse's *Eros and Civilisation*, despite the author's totalitarian tendencies.

eating) and life-inhibiting behaviour (e.g. war, suicide) are alternative ways of escaping from tension. Thus Freud's life instinct and death instinct find their common ground in Nirvana where happiness means a secure and carefree existence. This sounds to me very much like the Christian conception of heaven. But with communism, unlike heaven, you don't have to give up your life to get in—just your humanity.

Homer Lane used to have a little anecdote which illustrates the point I'm trying to make about the communist idea of happiness:

> "A dog and a rabbit are running down a field. Both apparently are doing the same thing, running and using their capacity to the full. Really there is a great difference between them. Their motives are different. One is happy, the other unhappy. The dog is happy because he is trying to do something with the hope of achieving it. The rabbit is unhappy because he is afraid. A few minutes later the position is reversed; the rabbit has reached his burrow and is inside panting, whilst the dog is sitting outside panting. The rabbit is now happy because it is safe, and therefore no longer afraid. The dog is unhappy because his hope has not been realised. Here we have the two kinds of happiness of which each one of us is capable—happiness based on the escape from danger, and happiness based on the fulfillment of a hope, which is the only true happiness."[30]

I leave it to the reader as an exercise in triviality to decide which of these two types of happiness is emphasised by communism. While on the subject of analogies, I'd like to indulge in one of my own. Generally speaking there are two kinds of cats: the "lap cat" and the "mouser." The former leads a peaceful existence, leaving granny's lap only long enough to make a discreet trip to its sandbox and to lap up a saucer of milk. The latter lives by catching mice in the farmer's barn and never goes near the inside of the farm house. The former is normally fat and lazy; the latter skinny and alert. Despite the lap cat's easier life, the mouser wouldn't exchange places with him if he could, while the lap cat COULDN'T exchange places if he would. Here we have two cats—perhaps even from the same litter—with two completely different attitudes toward life. The one expects a clean sandbox and food twice a day—and he is rarely disappointed. The other has to work for a living, but generally finds the reward worth while. "Now what has this got to do with the subject at hand?" I hear you cry. Just this: the communists would make "lap cats" of us all. "But what's so bad about that?" you may ask. To which I would have to reply (passing over the stinky problem of WHO will change the sandbox), "Have you ever tried to 'domesticate' a mouser?"

Communism, in its quest for a tranquil, tensionless world, inevitably harks back to the Middle Ages. Scratch a communist and chances are pretty good you'll find a mediaevalist underneath. Paul Goodman, for example, derives his ideal "community of scholars" from Bologna and Paris models based in the eleventh and twelfth centuries.[31] Erich Fromm writes longingly of "the sense of security which was characteristic of man in the Middle Ages....In having a distinct, unchangeable, and unquestionable place in the social world from the moment of birth, man was rooted in a structuralised whole, and thus life had a meaning which left no place, and no need, for doubt. A person was identical with his role in society; he was a peasant, an artisan, a knight, and not AN INDIVIDUAL who HAPPENED to have this or that occupation. The social order was conceived as a natural order, and being a definite part of it gave man a feeling of security and of belonging. There was comparatively little competition. One was born into a certain economic position which guaranteed a livelihood determined by tradition."[32] Kropotkin goes even further than Fromm. I'd like to examine his position in some detail because I think it is very instructive of how the communist mentality works. In perhaps his best-known book, *Mutual Aid*, Kropotkin devotes two of its eight chapters to glorifying the Middle Ages, which he boldly claim were one of "the two greatest periods of [mankind's] history."[33] (The other one being ancient Greece. He doesn't say how he reconciles this with the fact that Greece was based firmly on a foundation of slavery). "No period of history could better illustrate the constructive powers of the popular masses than the tenth and eleventh centuries...but, unhappily, this is a period about which historical information is especially scarce."[34] I wonder why? Could it be that everyone was having such a good time that no one found time to record it? Kropotkin writes of the mediaeval cities as "centres of liberty and enlightenment."[35] The mediaeval guilds, he says, answered "a deeply inrooted want of human nature,"[36] calling them "organisations for maintaining justice."[37] Let's see what Kropotkin means here by "justice":

> "If a brother's house is burned, or he has lost his ship, or has suffered on a pilgrim's voyage, all the brethren MUST come to his aid. If a brother falls dangerously ill, two brethren MUST keep watch by his bed till he is out of danger, and if he dies, the brethren must bury him—a great affair in those times of pestilences [Kropotkin must have been dozing to admit this in his Utopia]— and follow him to the church and the grave. After his death they MUST provide for his children....If a brother was involved in a quarrel with a stranger to the guild, they agreed to support him for bad and for good; that is, whether he was unjustly accused of aggression, OR REALLY WAS THE AGGRESSOR, they HAD to support him....They went to court to support by oath the truthfulness of his statements, and if he was found guilty they did not let him go to full ruin and become a slave through not paying the due compensation; they all paid it....Such were the leading ideas of those brotherhoods which gradually covered the whole of mediaeval life."[38]*

And such is Kropotkin's conception of "justice," which

---

*   Emphasis added.

could better be described as a warped sense of solidarity. He goes on to say, "It is evident that an institution so well suited to serve the need of union, without depriving the individual of his initiative, could but spread, grow, and fortify."[39]

"We see not only merchants, craftsmen, hunters, and peasants united in guilds; we also see guilds of priests, painters, teachers of primary schools and universities, guilds for performing the passion play, for building a church, for developing the 'mystery' of a given school of art or craft, or for a special recreation—even guilds among beggars, executioners, and lost women, all organised on the same double principle of self-jurisdiction and mutual support."[40] It was such "unity of thought" which Kropotkin thinks "can but excite our admiration."[41]

But where did the common labourer fit into all this? Kropotkin makes the remarkable generalisation that "at no time has labour enjoyed such conditions of prosperity and such respect."[42] As proof he cites the "glorious donations"[43] the workers gave to the cathedrals. These, he says, "bear testimony of their relative well-being."[44] (Just as the Taj Mahal bears testimony of the relative well-being of the people of India, no doubt). "Many aspirations of our modern radicals were already realised in the Middle Ages [and] much of what is described now as Utopian was accepted then as a matter of fact."[45]

As for the material achievements of the Middle Ages, Kropotkin can't find a superlative super enough to describe them—but he tries:

"The very face of Europe had been changed. The land was dotted with rich cities, surrounded by immense thick walls [I wonder why?] which were embellished by towers and gates, each of them a work of art in itself. The cathedrals, conceived in a grand style and profusely decorated, lifted their bell-towers to the skies, displaying a purity of form and a boldness of imagination which we now vainly strive to attain....[He displays a bit of 'boldness of imagination' himself (to be quite charitable) when he goes on to say:] Over large tracts of land well-being had taken the place of misery; learning had grown and spread. The methods of science had been elaborated; the basis of natural philosophy had been laid down; and the way had been paved for all the mechanical inventions of which our own times are so proud. Such were the magic [sic] changes accomplished in Europe in less than four hundred years."[46]

Just what were these "magic changes" of which Kropotkin is so proud? He lists about a dozen.[47] Among them are: printing (neglecting to inform us that the Gutenberg press was invented in the middle of the 15th century, sometime after the mediaeval cities "degenerated into centralised states"); steelmaking (neglecting to inform us that steelmaking had been mentioned in the works of Homer and was used continuously since that time); glassmaking (neglecting to inform us that the *Encyclopaedia Britannica*—to which he contributed numerous articles—devotes to the Middle Ages all of two sentences of a 27 page article on the history of glassmaking); the telescope (neglecting to inform us that it wasn't even invented until 1608); gunpowder and the compass (neglecting to inform us that the Chinese lay earlier claims to both of these inventions); algebra (neglecting to inform us that algebra was in common use in ancient Babylonia and that, although being introduced to mediaeval Europe by the Arabs, no important contributions were made by Europeans until the Renaissance); the decimal system (neglecting to inform us that the Hindus invented the system about a thousand years before it gained any ground in Europe in the 17th century); calendar reform (neglecting to inform us that although Roger Bacon suggested such reform to the Pope in the 13th century, no action was taken until 300 years later under the reign of Pope Gregory XIII in 1582); chemistry (neglecting to inform us of an earlier work of his where he said chemistry was "entirely a product of our [19th] century."[48]) Indeed the only things he mentions as products of the Middle Ages which stand up under scrutiny are counterpoint and, paradoxically, the mechanical clock. To top it all off, he then has the gall to cite Galileo and Copernicus as being "direct descendents" of mediaeval science[49]—somehow managing to ignore the fact that Galileo spent the last eight years of his life under house arrest for supporting the Copernican theory, thanks to that grand mediaeval institution, the Inquisition.

You may be wondering why the people of the Middle Ages let such a Utopia slip through their fingers. Kropotkin cites foreign invasions—notably those of the Mongols, Turks, and Moors[50]—but makes it quite clear that the "greatest and most fatal error of most cities was to bass their wealth upon commerce and industry."[51] So here we have it laid bare for all to see: Kropotkin's ideal community would not only return us to the dark ages, but would take away the one thing that could bring us back—commerce and industry.

Rudolf Rocker, the darling of the anarcho-syndicalists, similarly eulogises the Middle Ages. He, too, felt that mediaeval man led a "rich life"[52] which gave "wings to his spirit and prevent[ed] his mental stagnation."[53] But unlike Kropotkin—who chalked up mediaeval solidarity to man's innate "nature"—Rocker (correctly) explains these "fraternal associations" by means of a most unanarchistic concept—Christianity:

"Mediaeval man felt himself to be bound up with a single, uniform culture, a member of a great community extending over all countries, in whose bosom all people found their place. It was the community of Christendom which included all the scattered units of the Christian world and spiritually unified them....The deeper the concept of Christianity took root in men, the easier they overcame all barriers between themselves and others, and the stronger lived in them the consciousness that all belonged to one great community and strove toward a common goal."[54]

So we see that the glue that held these idyllic mediaeval communities together was not Kropotkin's "mutual aid," but rather Christian mysticism. Rocker was perceptive enough to see this; Kropotkin apparently was not. But what both of these men failed to see was that mysticism is the necessary glue of ANY communist society. The mystical Garden of Eden is the ultimate goal of every church of the communist religion. Unfortunately, as every good Christian will tell you, the only way you can stay in the Garden of Eden is to abstain from the "tree of knowledge." Communists are apparently willing to pay this price. Individualists are not. It is communism's intention to carry religion to its ultimate absurdity: it would sacrifice man on the cross of altruism for the sake of—Man.

I'd like to end my diatribe against communism by quoting another one. This is what one prophetic Frenchman, Pierre-Joseph Proudhon, had to say about communism eight years before the *Communist Manifesto* appeared like a spectre to haunt Europe—and like a good French wine, his words seem to have improved with age:

"Communism—or association in a simple form—is the necessary object and original aspiration of the social nature, the spontaneous movement by which it manifests and establishes itself. It is the first phase of human civilisation. In this state of society,—which the jurists have called 'negative communism',—man draws near to man, and shares with him the fruits of the field and the milk and flesh of animals. Little by little this communism—negative as long as man does not produce—tends to become positive and organic through the development of labour and industry. But it is then that the sovereignty of thought, and the terrible faculty of reasoning logically or illogically, teach man that, if equality is the sine qua non of society, communism is the first species of slavery....The disadvantages of communism are so obvious that its critics never have needed to employ much eloquence to thoroughly disgust men with it. The irreparability of the injustice which it causes, the violence which it does to attractions and repulsions, the yoke of iron which it fastens upon the will, the moral torture to which it subjects the conscience, the debilitating effect which it has upon society; and, to sum it all up, the pious and stupid uniformity which it enforces upon the free, active, reasoning, unsubmissive personality of man, have shocked common sense, and condemned communism by an irrevocable decree. The authorities and examples cited in its favour disprove it. The communistic republic of Plato involved slavery; that of Lycurgus employed Helots, whose duty it was to produce for their masters, thus enabling the latter to devote themselves exclusively to athletic sports and to war, Even J. J. Rousseau—confounding communism and equality—has said somewhere that, without slavery, he did not think equality of conditions possible. The communities of the early Church did not last the first century out, and soon degenerated into monasteries....The greatest danger to which society is exposed today is that of another shipwreck on this rock. Singularly enough, systematic communism— the deliberate negation of property—is conceived under the direct influence of the proprietary prejudice; and property is the basis of all communistic theories. The members of a community, it is true, have no private property; but the community is proprietor, and proprietor not only of the goods, but of the persons and wills. In consequence of this principle of absolute property, labour, which should be only a condition imposed upon man by Nature, becomes in all communities a human commandment, and therefore odious. Passive obedience, irreconcilable with a reflecting will, is strictly enforced. Fidelity to regulations, which are always defective, however wise they may be thought, allows of no complaint. Life, talent, and all the human faculties are the property of the State, which has the right to use them as it pleases for the common good. Private associations are sternly prohibited, in spite of the likes and dislikes of different natures, because to tolerate them would be to introduce small communities within the large one, and consequently private property; the strong work for the weak, although this ought to be left to benevolence, and not enforced, advised, or enjoined; the industrious work for the lazy though this is unjust; the clever work for the foolish, although this is absurd; and, finally, man—casting aside his personality, his spontaneity, his genius, and his affections—humbly annihilates himself at the feet of the majestic and inflexible Commune! Communism is inequality, but not as property is. Property is the exploitation of the weak by the strong. Communism is the exploitation of the strong by the weak. In property, inequality of conditions is the result of force, under whatever name it be disguised: physical and mental force; force of events, chance, FORTUNE; force of accumulated property, etc. In communism, inequality springs from placing mediocrity on a level with excellence. This damaging equation is repellent to the conscience, and causes merit to complain; for although it may be the duty of the strong to aid the weak, they prefer to do it out of generosity,—they never will endure a comparison. Give them equal opportunities of labour, and equal wages, but never allow their jealousy to be awakened by mutual suspicion of unfaithfulness in the performance of the common task. Communism is oppression and slavery. Man is very willing to obey the law of duty, serve his country, and oblige his friends; but he wishes to labour when he pleases, where he pleases, and as much as he pleases. He wishes to dispose of his own time, to be governed only by necessity, to choose his friendships, his recreation, and his discipline; to act from judgement, not by command; to sacrifice himself through selfishness, not through servile obligation. Communism is essentially opposed to the free exercise of our faculties, to our noblest desires, to our deepest feelings. Any plan which could be devised for reconciling it with the demands of the individual reason and will would end only in changing the thing while preserving the name. Now, if we are honest truth-seekers, we shall avoid disputes about words. Thus, communism violates the sovereignty of the conscience and equality: the first, by restricting spontaneity of mind and heart, and freedom of thought and action; the second, by placing labour and laziness, skill and stupidity, and even vice and virtue on an equality in point of comfort."[55]

---

*   See footnote on page 12.

REVOLUTION: THE ROAD TO FREEDOM?

"It's true that non-violence has been a dismal failure. The only bigger failure has been violence."

—JOAN BAEZ

There's an old story about a motorist who stopped a policeman in downtown Manhattan and asked him how he could get to the Brooklyn Bridge. The officer looked around, thought a minute, scratched his head and finally replied, "I'm sorry, but you can't get there from here." Some anarchists are now wondering if you can get to the free society from where we stand today. I must confess that I, too, harbour some doubts. But if there is a way, it is incumbent upon all who wish to find that way to carefully examine the important end-means problem.

"The end justifies the means." Few people would argue with this trite statement. Certainly all apologists of government must ultimately fall back on such reasoning to justify their large police forces and standing armies. Revolutionary anarchists must also rely on this argument to justify their authoritarian methods "just one more time", the revolution being for them "the unfreedom to end unfreedom." It seems that the only people who reject outright this article of faith are a handful of (mostly religious) pacifists. The question I'd like to consider here is not whether the end JUSTIFIES the means (because I, too, tend to feel that it does), but rather whether the end is AFFECTED by the means and, if so, to what extent.

That the end is affected by the means should be obvious. Whether I obtain your watch by swindling you, buying it from you, stealing it from you, or soliciting it as a gift from you makes the same watch "graft", "my property", "booty", or "a donation." The same can be said for social change. Even so strong an advocate of violent revolution as Herbert Marcuse, in one of his rare lapses into sanity, realised this fact:

"Unless the revolution itself progresses through freedom, the need for domination and repression would be carried over into the new society and the fateful separation between the 'immediate' and the 'true' interest of the individuals would be almost inevitable; the individuals would become the objects of their own liberation, and freedom would be a matter of administration and decree. Progress would be progressive repression, and the 'delay' in freedom would threaten to become self-propelling and self-perpetuating."[56]

But despite the truth of Marcuse's observation, we still find many anarchists looking for a shortcut to freedom by means of violent revolution. The idea that anarchism can be inaugurated by violence is as fallacious as the idea that it can be sustained by violence. The best that can be said for violence is that it may, in rare circumstances, be used as an expedient to save us from extinction. But the individualist's rejection of violence (except in cases of self-defence) is not due to any lofty pacifist principles; it's a matter of pure pragmatism: we realise that violence just simply does not work.

The task of anarchism, as the individualist sees it, is not to destroy the state, but rather to destroy the MYTH of the state. Once people realise that they no longer need the state, it will—in the words of Frederick Engels—inevitably "wither away" (*Anti-Duehring*, 1877) and be consigned to the "Museum of Antiquities, by the side of the spinning wheel and the bronze axe" (*Origin of the Family, Private Property and the State*, 1884). But unless anarchists can create a general and well-grounded disbelief in the state as an INSTITUTION, the existing state might be destroyed by violent revolution or it might fall through its own rottenness, but another would inevitably rise in its place. And why shouldn't it? As long as people believe the state to be necessary (even a "necessary evil", as Thomas Paine said), the state will always exist.

We have already seen how Kropotkin would usher in the millennium by the complete expropriation of all property.

"We must see clearly in private property what it really is, a conscious or unconscious robbery of the substance of all, and seize it joyfully for the common benefit."[57] He cheerfully goes on to say, "The instinct of destruction, so natural and so just...will find ample room for satisfaction."[58] Kropotkin's modern-day heirs are no different. Noam Chomsky, writing in the "New York Review of Books" and reprinted in a recent issue of *Anarchy*, applauds the heroism of the Paris Commune of 1871, mentioning only in passing that "the Commune, of course [!], was drowned in blood."[59] Later in the same article he writes, "What is far more important is that these ideas [direct workers' control] have been realised in spontaneous revolutionary action, for example in Germany and Italy after World War I and in Spain (specifically, industrial Barcelona) in 1936."[60] What Chomsky apparently finds relatively UNimportant are the million-odd corpses which were the direct result of these "spontaneous revolutionary actions." He also somehow manages to ignore the fact that the three countries he mentions—Germany, Italy and Spain— were without exception victims of fascism within a few years of these glorious revolutions. One doesn't need a great deal of insight to be able to draw a parallel between these "spontaneous" actions with their reactionary aftermaths and the spontaneous "trashings" which are currently in fashion in the United States. But it seems the Weathermen really DO "need a weatherman to know which way the wind blows."[61]

The question of how to attain the anarchist society has divided anarchists nearly as much as the question of what the anarchist society actually is. While Bakunin insisted on the necessity of "bloody revolutions"[62], Proudhon believed that violence was unnecessary—saying instead that "reason will serve us better."[63] The same discord was echoed on the other side of the Atlantic some decades later when, in the wake of the infamous Haymarket bombing, the issue of violence came to a head. Benjamin Tucker, writing in the columns of *Liberty*, had this to say about accusations leveled against him by Johann Most, the communist-anarchist editor of *Freiheit*:

"It makes very little difference to Herr Most what a man believes in economics. The test of fellowship with him lies in acceptance of dynamite as a cure-all. Though I should prove that my economic views, if realised, would turn our social system inside out, he would not therefore regard me as a revolutionist. He declares outright that I am no revolutionist, because the thought of the coming revolution (by dynamite, he means) makes my flesh creep. Well, I frankly confess that I take no pleasure in the thought of bloodshed and mutilation and death. At these things my feelings revolt. And if delight in them is a requisite of a revolutionist, then indeed I am no revolutionist. When revolutionist and cannibal become synonyms, count me out, if you please. But, though my feelings revolt, I am not mastered by them or made a coward by them. More than from dynamite and blood do I shrink from the thought of a permanent system of society involving the slow starvation of the most industrious and deserving of its members. If I should ever become convinced that the policy of bloodshed is necessary to end our social system, the loudest of today's shriekers for blood would not surpass me in the stoicism with which I would face the inevitable. Indeed, a plumb-liner to the last, I am confident that under such circumstances many who now think me chicken-hearted would condemn the stony-heartedness with which I should favour the utter sacrifice of every feeling of pity to the necessities of the terroristic policy. Neither fear nor sentimentalism, then, dictates my opposition to forcible methods. Such being the case, how stupid, how unfair, in Herr Most, to picture me as crossing myself at the mention of the word revolution simply because I steadfastly act on my well-known belief that force cannot substitute truth for a lie in political economy!"[64]

It is this issue of economics which generally sorts anarchists into the violent and non-violent wings of anarchism.

Individualists, by and large, are pacifists in practice (if not in theory), whereas the communists tend toward violent revolution.* Why is this so? One reason I think is that individualists are more concerned with changing the conditions which directly affect their lives than they are with reforming the whole world "for the good of all." The communists, on the other hand, have a more evangelical spirit. Like all good missionaries, they are out to convert the unbeliever—whether he likes it or not. And inevitably this leads to violence. Another reason communists are more prone to violence than individualists can be found, I think, in looking at the nature of the force each is willing to use to secure and sustain his respective system. Individualists believe that the only justifiable force is force used in preventing invasion (i.e. defensive force). Communists, however, would compel the worker to pool his products with the products of others and forbid him to sell his labour or the products of his labour. To "compel" and "forbid" requires the use of offensive force. It is no wonder, then, that most communists advocate violence to achieve their objectives.

If freedom is really what we anarchists crack it up to be, it shouldn't be necessary to force it down the throat of anyone. What an absurdity! Even so superficial a writer as Agatha Christie recognised that "if it is not possible to go back [from freedom], or to choose to go back, then it is not freedom."[66] A. J. Muste used to say that "there is no way to peace—peace IS the way." The same thing is true about freedom: the only way to freedom is BY freedom. This statement is so nearly tautological that it should not need saying. The only way to realise anarchy is for a sufficient number of people to be convinced that their own interests demand it. Human society does not run on idealism—it runs on pragmatism. And unless people can be made to realise that anarchy actually

---

*   There are exceptions of course. It is hard to imagine a more dedicated pacifist than Tolstoy, for example. On the other side of the coin is Stirner, who quotes with near relish the French Revolutionary slogan "the world will have no rest till the last king is hanged with the guts of the last priest."[65]

works for THEIR benefit, it will remain what it is today: an idle pipe dream; "a nice theory, but unrealistic." It is the anarchist's job to convince people otherwise.

Herbert Spencer—the great evolutionist of whom Darwin said, "He is about a dozen times my superior"—observed the following fact of nature:

> "Metamorphosis is the universal law, exemplified throughout the Heavens and on the Earth: especially throughout the organic world; and above all in the animal division of it. No creature, save the simplest and most minute, commences its existence in a form like that which it eventually assumes; and in most cases the unlikeness is great—so great that kinship between the first and the last forms would be incredible were it not daily demonstrated in every poultry-yard and every garden. More than this is true. The changes of form are often several: each of them being an apparently complete transformation—egg, larva, pupa, imago, for example ... No one of them ends as it begins; and the difference between its original structure and its ultimate structure is such that, at the outset change of the one into the other would have seemed incredible."[67]

This universal law of metamorphosis holds not only for biology, but for society as well. Modern-day Christianity resembles the early Christian church about as much as a butterfly resembles a caterpillar. Thomas Jefferson would have been horrified if he could have foreseen the "government by the consent of the governed" which today is the hereditary heir of his Declaration of Independence. French revolutionaries took turns beheading one another until that great believer in "les droits de l'homme", Napoleon Bonaparte, came upon the scene to secure "liberté, égalité, fraternité" for all. And wasn't it comrade Stalin who in 1906 so confidently forecast the nature of the coming revolution?: "The dictatorship of the proletariat will be a dictatorship of the entire proletariat as a class over the bourgeoisie and not the domination of a few

individuals over the proletariat."[68] The examples of these ugly duckling stories in reverse are endless. For as Robert Burns wrote nearly two centuries ago:
"The best laid schemes o' mice and men Gang aft a-gley; An' lea'e us nought but grief and pain For promis'd joy."[69]

Why is it that Utopian dreams have a habit of turning into nightmares in practice? Very simply because people don't act the way the would-be architects of society would have them act. The mythical man never measures up to the real man. This point was brought home forcefully in a recent letter to *Freedom* by S. E. Parker who observed that our modern visionaries are bound for disappointment because they are "trying to deduce an 'is' from an 'ought.'"[70] Paper constitutions might work all right in a society of paper dolls, but they can only bring smiles to those who have observed their results in the real world. The same is true of paper revolutions which invariably have to go back to the drawing board once the reign of terror sets in. And if communist-anarchists think that their paper social systems are exempt from this, how do they explain the presence of anarchist "leaders" in high government positions during the Spanish Civil War?

Hasn't everyone been surprised at sometime or other with the behaviour of people they thought they knew well? Perhaps a relative or a good friend does something "totally out of character." We can never completely know even those people closest to us, let alone total strangers. How are we, then, to comprehend and predict the behaviour of complex groups of people? To make assumptions about how people must and will act under a hypothetical social system is idle conjecture. We know from daily experience that men don't act as they "ought" to act or think as they "ought" to think. Why should things be any different after the revolution? Yet we still find an abundance of revolutionaries willing to kill and be killed for a cause which more likely than not, if realised, would bear no recognizable resemblance to what they were fighting for. This reason alone should be sufficient to give these people second thoughts about their methods. But apparently they are too carried away by the violence of their own rhetoric to be bothered with where it will lead them.*

There is but one effective way to rid ourselves of the oppressive power of the state. It is not to shoot it to death; it is not to vote it to death; it is not even to persuade it to death. It is rather to starve it to death.

Power feeds on its spoils, and dies when its victims refuse to be despoiled. There is much truth in the well-known pacifist slogan, "Wars will cease when people refuse to fight." This slogan can be generalised to say that "government will cease when people refuse to be governed." As Tucker put it, "There is not a tyrant in the civilised world today who would not do anything in his power to precipitate a bloody revolution rather than see himself confronted by any large fraction of his subjects determined not to obey. An insurrection is easily quelled; but no army is willing or able to train its guns on inoffensive people who do not even gather in the streets but stay at home and stand back on their rights."[71]

A particularly effective weapon could be massive tax refusal. If (say) one-fifth of the population of the United States refused to pay their taxes, the government would be impaled on the horns of a dilemma. Should they ignore the problem, it would only get worse—for who is going to willingly contribute to the government's coffers when his neighbours are getting away scotfree? Or should they opt to prosecute, the burden just to feed and guard so many "parasites"—not to mention the loss of revenue—would be so great that the other four-fifths of the population would soon rebel. But in order to succeed, this type of action would require massive numbers. Isolated tax refusal—like isolated draft refusal—is a useless waste of resources. It is like trying to purify the

---

* I am reminded here of a Herblock cartoon which came out during the Johnson-Goldwater presidential campaign of 1964. It pictures Goldwater standing in the rubble of a nuclear war and proclaiming, "But that's not what I meant!" I wonder if the Utopia which our idealists intend to usher in by violent revolution will be what they really "meant"?

salty ocean by dumping a cup of distilled water into it. The individualist-anarchist would no more advocate such sacrificial offerings than the violent revolutionary would advocate walking into his neighbourhood police station and "offing the pig." As he would tell you, "It is not wise warfare to throw your ammunition to the enemy unless you throw it from the cannon's mouth." Tucker agrees. Replying to a critic who felt otherwise he said, "Placed in a situation where, from the choice of one or the other horn of a dilemma, it must follow either that fools will think a man a coward or that wise men will think him a fool, I can conceive of no possible ground for hesitancy in the selection."[72]

There is a tendency among anarchists these days—particularly in the United States—to talk about "alternatives" and "parallel institutions". This is a healthy sign which individualists very much encourage. The best argument one can possibly present against "the system" is to DEMONSTRATE a better one. Some communist-anarchists (let it be said to their credit) are now trying to do just that. Communal farms, schools, etc. have been sprouting up all over the States. Individualists, of course, welcome these experiments—especially where they fulfill the needs of those involved and contribute to their happiness. But we can't help questioning the over-all futility of such social landscape gardening. The vast majority of these experiments collapse in dismal failure within the first year or two, proving nothing but the difficulty of communal living. And should an isolated community manage to survive, their success could not be judged as conclusive since it would be said that their principles were applicable only to people well-nigh perfect. They might well be considered as the exceptions which proved the rule. If anarchy is to succeed to any appreciable extent, it has to be brought within the reach of everyone. I'm afraid that tepees in New Mexico don't satisfy that criterion.

The parallel institution I would like to see tried would be

something called a "mutual bank."* The beauty of this proposal is that it can be carried out under the very nose of the man-in-the-street. I would hope that in this way people could see for themselves the practical advantages it has to offer them, and ultimately accept the plan as their own. I'm well aware that this scheme, like any other, is subject to the law of metamorphosis referred to earlier. But should this plan fail, unlike those plans which require bloody revolutions for their implementation, the only thing hurt would be the pride of a few hair-brained individualists.

---

* The reader can judge for himself the merits of this plan when I examine it in some detail later on in this article.

EGOISM: THE PHILOSOPHY OF FREEDOM

"Many a year I've used my nose To smell the onion and the rose; Is there any proof which shows That I've a right to that same nose?"
—JOHANN CHRISTOPH FRIEDRICH SCHILLER

The philosophy of individualist-anarchism is "egoism." It is not my purpose here to give a detailed account of this philosophy, but I would like to explode a few of the more common myths about egoism and present to the reader enough of its essence so that he may understand more clearly the section on individualist economics. I am tempted here to quote long extracts from *The Ego and His Own*, for it was this book which first presented the egoist philosophy in a systematic way. Unfortunately, I find that Stirner's "unique" style does not readily lend itself to quotation. So what I have done in the following pages is to dress up Stirner's ideas in a language largely my own.

Voltaire once said, "If God did not exist, it would be necessary to invent him." Bakunin wisely retorted, "If God DID exist, it would be necessary to abolish him." Unfortunately, Bakunin would only abolish God. It is the egoist's intention to abolish GODS. It is clear from Bakunin's writings that what he meant by God was what Voltaire meant—namely the religious God. The egoist sees many more gods than that—in fact, as many as there are fixed ideas. Bakunin's gods, for example, include the god of humanity, the god of brotherhood, the god of mankind—all variants on the god of altruism. The egoist, in striking down ALL gods, looks only to his WILL. He recognises no legitimate power over himself.*

---

*   He does not, of course, claim to be omnipotent. There ARE external powers over him. The difference between the egoist and non-egoist in this

The world is there for him to consume—if he CAN. And he can if he has the power. For the egoist, the only right is the right of might. He accepts no "inalienable rights," for such rights—by virtue of the fact that they're inalienable—must come from a higher power, some god. The American Declaration of Independence, for example, in proclaiming these rights found it necessary to invoke the "Laws of Nature and of Nature's God." The same was true of the French Revolutionary "Déclaration des droits de l'homme et du citoyen."

The egoist recognises no right—or what amounts to the same thing—claims ALL rights for himself. What he can get by force he has a right to; and what he can't, he has no right. He demands no rights, nor does he recognise them in others. "Right—is a wheel in the head, put there by a spook,"[73] says Stirner. Right is also the spook which has kept men servile throughout the ages. The believer in rights has always been his own jailer. What sovereign could last the day out without a general belief in the "divine right of kings"? And where would Messrs. Nixon, Heath, et. al. be today without the "right" of the majority?

Men make their tyrants as they make their gods. The tyrant is a man like any other. His power comes from the abdicated power of his subjects. If people believe a man to have superhuman powers, they automatically GIVE him those powers by default. Had Hitler's pants fallen down during one of his ranting speeches, the whole course of history might have been different. For who can respect a naked Fuehrer? And who knows? The beginning of the end of Lyndon Johnson's political career might well have been when he showed his operation scar on coast-to-coast television for the whole wide world to see that he really was a man after all. This sentiment was expressed by Stirner when he said, "Idols exist through me; I need only refrain from creating them anew, then they exist no longer: 'higher powers' exist only through my exalt-

---

regard is therefore one mainly of attitude: the egoist recognises external power as an enemy and consciously fights against it, while the non-egoist humbles himself before it and often accepts it as a friend.

ing them and abasing myself. Consequently my relation to the world is this: I no longer do anything for it 'for God's sake,' I do nothing 'for man's sake,' but what I do I do 'for my sake.'"[74] The one thing that makes a man different from any other living creature is his power to reason. It is by this power that man can (and does) dominate over the world. Without reason man would be a pathetic non-entity—evolution having taken care of him long before the dinosaur. Now some people say that man is by nature a social animal, something like an ant or a bee. Egoists don't deny the sociability of man, but what we do say is that man is sociable to the extent that it serves his own self-interest. Basically man is (by nature, if you will) a selfish being. The evidence for this is overwhelming.* Let us look at a hive of bees to see what would happen if "reason" were suddenly introduced into their lives:

"In the first place, the bees would not fail to try some new industrial process; for instance, that of making their cells round or square. All sorts of systems and inventions would be tried, until long experience, aided by geometry, should show them that the hexagonal shape is the best. Then insurrections would occur. The drones would be told to provide for themselves, and the queens to labour; jealousy would spread among the labourers; discords would burst forth; soon each one would want to produce on his own account; and finally the hive would be abandoned, and the bees would perish. Evil would be introduced into the honey-producing republic by the power of reflection,—the very faculty which ought to constitute its glory."[75]

So it would appear to me that reason would militate against blind, selfless cooperation. But by the same token, reason leads to cooperation which is mutually beneficial to all parties concerned. Such cooperation is what Stirner called a "union of egoists."[76] This binding together is not done through any innate social instinct, but rather as a mat-

---

* Many people cite trade unions as a "proof" of man's solidarity and sociability. Just the opposite is true. Why else do people strike if not for their own "selfish" ends, e.g. higher wages, better working conditions, shorter hours?

ter of individual convenience. These unions would probably take the form of contracting individuals. The object of these contracts not being to enable all to benefit equally from their union (although this isn't ruled out, the egoist thinks it highly unlikely), but rather to protect one another from invasion and to secure to each contracting individual what is mutually agreed upon to be "his."

By referring to a man's selfishness, you know where you stand. Nothing is done "for free." Equity demands reciprocity. Goods and services are exchanged for goods and services or (what is equivalent) bought. This may sound "heartless"— but what is the alternative? If one depends on kindness, pity or love the services and goods one gets become "charity." The receiver is put in the position of a beggar, offering nothing in return for each "present." If you've ever been on the dole, or know anyone who has, you will know that the receiver of such gifts is anything but gracious. He is stripped of his manhood and he resents it. Now the egoist isn't (usually) so cold and cruel as this description makes him out to be. As often as not he is as charitable and kind as his altruist neighbour. But he CHOOSES the objects of his kindness; he objects to COMPULSORY "love." What an absurdity! If love were universal, it would have no meaning. If I should tell my wife that I love her because I love humanity, I would be insulting her. I love her not because she happens to be a member of the human race, but rather for what she is to me. For me she is something special: she possesses certain qualities which I admire and which make me happy. If she is unhappy, I suffer, and therefore I try to comfort her and cheer her up—for MY sake. Such love is a selfish love. But it is the only REAL love. Anything else is an infatuation with an image, a ghost. As Stirner said of his loved ones, "I love them with the consciousness of egoism; I love them because love makes ME happy, I love because loving is natural to me, because it pleases me. I know no 'commandment of love'."[77]

The lover of "humanity" is bewitched by a superstition. He has dethroned God, only to accept the reign of the holy trinity: Morality, Conscience and Duty. He becomes a "true believer"—a religious man. No longer believing in himself, he becomes a slave to Man. Then, like all religious men, he is overcome with feelings of "right" and "virtue." He becomes a soldier in the service of humanity whose intolerance of heretics rivals that of the most righteous religious fanatic. Most of the misery in the world today (as in the past) is directly attributable to men acting "for the common good." The individual is nothing; the mass all.

The egoist would reverse this situation. Instead of everyone looking after the welfare of everyone else, each would look after his own welfare. This would, in one fell swoop, do away with the incredibly complicated, wasteful and tyrannical machinery (alluded to previously) necessary to see to it that not only everyone got his fair share of the communal pie, but that everyone contributed fairly to its production. In its stead we egoists raise the banner of free competition: "the war of all against all" as the communists put it. But wouldn't that lead to (dare I say it) ANARCHY? Of course it would. What anarchist would deny the logical consequences of the principles he advocates? But let's see what this "anarchy" would be like.

The egoist believes that the relationships between men who are alive to their own individual interests would be far more just and equitable than they are now. Take the property question for example. Today there is a great disparity of income. Americans make up about 7% of the world's population, but they control over half of its wealth. And among the Americans, nearly one quarter of the wealth is owned by 5% of the people.[78] Such unequal distribution of wealth is due primarily to the LEGAL institution of property. Without the state to back up legal privilege and without the people's acquiescence to the privileged minority's legal right to that property, these disparities would soon disappear. For what makes the rich man rich and the poor man poor if not the

---

* Contrary to popular belief, this gulf is getting larger. Since 1966, despite a constantly mushrooming GNP, the American factory workers' REAL wages (as opposed to his apparent, inflationary wages) have actually declined.[79]

latter GIVING the former the product of his labour?

Stirner is commonly thought to have concerned himself little with the economic consequences of his philosophy. It is true that he avoided elaborating on the exact nature of his "union of egoists," saying that the only way of knowing what a slave will do when he breaks his chains is to wait and see. But to say that Stirner was oblivious to economics is just not so. On the contrary. It was he, after all, who translated into German both Adam Smith's classic *An Inquiry into the Nature and Causes of the Wealth of Nations* and Jean Baptiste Say's pioneering work on the free market economy, *Traité d'économie politique*. The few pages he devotes to economics in *The Ego and His Own* are among his best:

> "If we assume that, as ORDER belongs to the essence of the State, so SUBORDINATION too is founded in its nature, then we see that the subordinates, or those who have received preferment, disproportionately OVER-CHARGE and OVERREACH those who are put in the lower ranks....By what then is your property secure, you creatures of preferment?...By our refraining from interference! And so by OUR protection! And what do you give us for it? Kicks and disdain you give to the 'common people'; police supervision, and a catechism with the chief sentence 'Respect what is NOT YOURS, what belongs to OTHERS! respect others, and especially your superiors!' But we reply, 'If you want our respect, BUY it for a price agreeable to us. We will leave you your property, if you give a due equivalent for this leaving.'... What equivalent do you give for our chewing potatoes and looking calmly on while you swallow oysters? Only buy the oysters of us as dear as we have to buy the potatoes of you, then you may go on eating them. Or do you suppose the oysters do not belong to us as much as to you?...Let us consider our nearer property, labour...We distress ourselves twelve hours in the sweat of our face, and you offer us a few pennies for it. Then take the like

for your labour too. Are you not willing? You fancy that our labour is richly repaid with that wage, while yours on the other hand is worth a wage of many thousands. But, if you did not rate yours so high, and gave us a better chance to realise value from ours, then we might well, if the case demanded it, bring to pass still more important things than you do for the many thousand pounds; and, if you got only such wages as we, you would soon grow more industrious in order to receive more. But, if you render any service that seems to us worth ten and a hundred times more than our own labour, why, then you shall get a hundred times more for it too; we, on the other hand, think also to produce for you things for which you will requite us more highly than with the ordinary day's wages. We shall be willing to get along with each other all right, if only we have first agreed on this—that neither any longer needs to—PRESENT anything to the other....We want nothing presented by you, but neither will we present you with anything. For centuries we have handed alms to you from good-hearted—stupidity, have doled out the mite of the poor and given to the masters the things that are—not the masters'; now just open your wallet, for henceforth our ware rises in price quite enormously. We do not want to take from you anything, anything at all, only you are to pay better for what you want to have. What then have you? 'I have an estate of a thousand acres.' And I am your plowman, and will henceforth attend to your fields only for a full day's wages. 'Then I'll take another.' You won't find any, for we plowmen are no longer doing otherwise, and, if one puts in an appearance who takes less, then let him beware of us. There is the housemaid, she too is now demanding as much, and you will no longer find one below this price. 'Why, then it is all over with me.' Not so fast! You will doubtless take in as much as we; and, if it should not be so, we will take off so much that you shall have wherewith to live like us. 'But I am accustomed to live better.'

We have nothing against that, but it is not our lookout; if you can clear more, go ahead. Are we to hire out under rates, that you may have a good living? The rich man always puts off the poor with the words, 'What does your want concern me? See to it how you make your way through the world; that is YOUR AFFAIR, not mine.' Well, let us let it be our affair, then, and let us not let the means that we have to realise value from ourselves be pilfered from us by the rich. 'But you uncultured people really do not need so much.' Well, we are taking somewhat more in order that for it we may procure the culture that we perhaps need....'O ill-starred equality!' No, my good old sir, nothing of equality. We only want to count for what we are worth, and, if you are worth more, you shall count for more right along. We only want to be WORTH OUR PRICE, and think to show ourselves worth the price that you will pay."[80]

Fifty years later Benjamin Tucker took over where Stirner left off:

"The minute you remove privilege, the class that now enjoy it will be forced to sell their labour, and then, when there will be nothing but labour with which to buy labour, the distinction between wage-payers and wage-receivers will be wiped out, and every man will be a labourer exchanging with fellow-labourers. Not to abolish wages, but to make EVERY man dependent upon wages and secure to every man his WHOLE wages is the aim of Anarchistic Socialism. What Anarchistic Socialism aims to abolish is usury. It does not want to deprive labour of its reward; it wants to deprive capital of its reward. It does not hold that labour should not be sold; it holds that capital should not be hired at usury."[81]

Franklin D. Roosevelt said in his second inaugural address that "We have always known that heedless self-interest was bad morals; we know now that it is bad economics." I've tried to show in this section that self-interest is "good morals." I now intend to show that it is also good economics.

CAPITALISM: FREEDOM PERVERTED

"Permit me to issue and control the money of a nation and I care not who makes its laws."
—MEYER A. ROTHCHILD

Roosevelt, in blaming the depression of the 'thirties on "heedless self-interest," played a cheap political trick for which the world has been suffering ever since. The great crash of 1929, far from being created by "free enterprise," was created by government interference in the free market. The Federal Reserve Board had been artificially controlling interest rates since 1913. The tax structure of the country was set up in such a way as to encourage ridiculously risky speculation in the stock market. "Protective tariffs" destroyed anything that vaguely resembled a free market. Immigration barriers prevented the free flow of the labour market. Anti-trust laws threatened prosecution for charging less than the competition ("intent to monopolise") and for charging the same as the competition ("price fixing"), but graciously permitted charging more than the competition (commonly called "going out of business.") With all these legislative restraints and controls, Roosevelt still had the gall to blame the depression on the "free" market economy. But what was his answer to the "ruthlessness" of freedom? This is what he had to say on taking office in 1933:

> "If we are to go forward, we must move as a trained and loyal army willing to sacrifice to the good of a common discipline, because without such discipline no progress is made, no leadership becomes effective. We are, I know, ready and willing to submit our lives and property to such discipline because it makes possible a leadership which aims at a larger good."[82]

We've been on that Keynesian road ever since. The "larger good" has become larger and larger until today the only cure the politicians come up with for the economy's ills is more of the same poison which made it sick in the first place. The rationale for such a policy was expressed by G. D. H. Cole in 1933:

> "If once a departure is made from the classical method of letting all the factors [of the economy] alone—and we have seen enough of that method [have we?] to be thoroughly dissatisfied with it—it becomes necessary to control ALL the factors...for interference with one, while the others are left unregulated, is certain to result in a fatal lack of balance in the working of the economic system.."[83]*

Many people, on hearing the individualist critique of governmental control of the economy, jump to the erroneous conclusion that we believe in capitalism. I'm sorry to say that some anarchists—who should know better—share this common fallacy. In a letter to "Freedom" a few months ago I tried to clear up this myth. Replying to an article by one of its editors, I had this to say:

> "First let me look at the term 'anarcho-capitalist.' This, it seems to me, is just an attempt to slander the individualist-anarchists by using a supercharged word like 'capitalist' in much the same way as the word 'anarchy' is popularly used to mean chaos and disorder. No one to my knowledge accepts the anarcho-capitalist label", just as no one up to the time of Proudhon's memoir on property in 1840 accepted the anarchist label. But, unlike

---

*   Emphasis added.

**   I have since been informed that "the term 'anarcho-capitalist' is now in use in the USA—particularly amongst those who contribute to the Los Angeles publication 'Libertarian Connection.'" It seems to me that people accepting such a label must do so primarily for its shock value. Very few people like capitalists these days, and those who do certainly don't like anarchists. What better term could you find to offend everyone?

Proudhon who could call himself an anarchist by stripping the word of its derogatory connotation and looking at its real MEANING, no one can logically call himself an anarcho-capitalist for the simple reason that it's a contradiction in terms: anarchists seek the abolition of the state while capitalism is inherently dependent upon the state. Without the state, capitalism would inevitably fall, for capitalism rests on the pillars of government privilege. Because of government a privileged minority can monopolise land, limit credit, restrict exchange, give idle capital the power to increase, and, through interest, rent, profit, and taxes, rob industrious labour of its products."[84]

Now most anarchists when they attack capitalism strike it where it is strongest: in its advocacy of freedom. And how paradoxical that is. Here we have the anarchists, champions of freedom PAR EXCELLENCE, complaining about freedom! How ridiculous, it seems to me, to find anarchists attacking Mr. Heath for withdrawing government subsidies from museums and children's milk programmes. When anarchists start screaming for free museums, free milk, free subways, free medical care, free education, etc., etc., they only show their ignorance of what freedom really is. All these "free" goodies which governments so graciously shower upon their subjects ultimately come from the recipients themselves—in the form of taxes. Governments are very clever at concealing just how large this sum actually is. They speak of a billion pounds here and a few hundred million dollars there. But what does a figure like $229,232,000,000.00 (Nixon's proposed budget) actually mean to the taxpayer? Virtually nothing. It's just a long string of numbers preceded by a dollar sign. People have no conception of numbers that size. But let me try to shed some light on this figure by breaking it down into a number the individual taxpayer can't help but understand: the average annual cost per family. This is a number governments NEVER talk about—for if they did, there would be a revolt which would make the storming of the Bastille look like a Sunday school picnic. Here's how to calculate it: you take the government's annual budget and divide it by the population of the country; then you multiply the result by the average size of family (4.5 seems a reasonable number). Doing this for the American case cited, we come to $4,800 (i.e. 2000 pounds per family per year!*). And that is just the FEDERAL tax bite. State and local taxes (which primarily pay for America's "free" education and "free" public highways) have yet to be considered. I leave it as an exercise to the British reader to see why their "welfare state" also prefers to mask budgetary figures by using astronomical numbers.

One thing should be clear from this example: nothing is for nothing. But the Santa Claus myth dies hard, even—or should I say especially?—among anarchists. The only encouraging sign to the contrary I have found in the anarchist press of late was when Ian Sutherland complained in the columns of *Freedom*: "I object, strongly, to having a large section of my 'product', my contribution to society, forcibly removed from me by a paternalistic state to dispense to a fool with 10 kids."[85] Unfortunately, I suspect that Mr Sutherland would only replace the "paternalistic state" by the "paternalistic commune"—and in so doing would still end up supporting those 10 kids. My suspicions were nourished by what he said in the very next paragraph about "laissez faire" anarchists: "perhaps they should join the Powellites." Perhaps Mr Sutherland should learn what laissez faire means.

Laissez faire is a term coined by the French physiocrats during the eighteenth century. John Stuart Mill brought it into popular English usage with the publication in 1848 of his *Principles of Political Economy*, where he examined the arguments for and against government intervention in the economy. The "con" side of the argument he called laissez faire. "The principle of 'laissez faire' in economics calls for perfect freedom in production; distribution of the returns

---

*   I am usually quite conservative in my use of exclamation marks. When I used this example in a recent letter to "Freedom", the editors saw fit to insert one where I had not. In keeping with their precedent, I will do likewise.

(or profit) to the factors of production according to the productivity of each; and finally, markets in which prices are determined by the free interplay of forces that satisfy buyers and sellers."[86] I find it difficult to see how any advocate of freedom could possibly object to a doctrine like this one. Unfortunately, what happened in the 19th century was that a handful of capitalists, who were anything but believers if freedom, picked up this nice sounding catch phrase and decided to "improve" upon it. These "improvements" left them with the freedom to exploit labour but took away labour's freedom to exploit capital. These capitalists, in perverting the original meaning of laissez faire, struck a blow against freedom from which it still suffers to this day. The capitalist who advocates laissez faire is a hypocrite. If he really believed in freedom, he could not possibly condone the greatest invader of freedom known to man: government. The capitalist necessarily relies on government to protect his privileged RIGHTS. Let us look at the foremost advocate of capitalism today, Ayn Rand. Her book "Capitalism: The Unknown Ideal" has two appendices. The first is on "Man's Rights" where she say, "INDIVIDUAL RIGHTS ARE THE MEANS OF SUBORDINATING SOCIETY TO MORAL LAW."[87*] Once again we are back to "rights" and "morals" which Stirner so strongly warned us about. And where does this lead us? Directly to Appendix Two, "The Nature of Government," where she says that government is "necessary" because "men need an institution charged with the task of protecting [you guessed it] their rights."[88] Let's see what some of these precious rights are:

I. Chapter 11 of Miss Rand's book is devoted to a defence of patent and copyright laws. In it she calls upon government to "certify the origination of an idea and protect its owner's exclusive right to use and disposal."[89] Realising the absurdity of PERPETUAL property in ideas ("consider what would happen if, in producing an automobile, we had to pay royalties to the descendants of all the inventors involved, starting with the inventor of the wheel and on up."[90]), she goes into

---

*   Her emphasis.

considerable mental acrobatics to justify intellectual property for a LIMITED time. But by so doing, she only succeeds in arousing our suspicion of her motives, for it seems strange that a mere lapse of time should negate something so precious as a man's "right" to his property. Admitting that "a patented invention often tends to hamper or restrict further research and development in a given area of science[91], our champion of the unhampered economy nevertheless manages to justify governmental "protection" to secure the inventor's "rights." As for copyrights, our millionaire author thinks "the most rational" length of time for this governmental protection would be "for the lifetime of the author and fifty years thereafter."[92] How does she justify all this? The way she justifies most of her inane arguments—by quoting herself: "Why should Rearden be the only one permitted to manufacture Rearden Metal?"[93] Why indeed?

II. Capitalists are fond of proclaiming the "rights" of private property. One of their favourite property rights is the right to own land without actually occupying it. The only way this can possibly be done is, once again, by government protection of legal pieces of paper called "titles" and "deeds." Without these scraps of paper, vast stretches of vacant land would be open to those who could use them and exorbitant rent could no longer be extracted from the non-owning user as tribute to the non-using owner.

There is much talk these days of a "population explosion." It is claimed that land is becoming more and more scarce and that by the year such and such there will be 38.2 people per square inch of land. But just how scarce is land? If all the world's land were divided up equally, every individual would have more than ten acres apiece. Even "crowded" islands like Britain and Japan have more than an acre per person on average.[94] When you consider how few people actually own any of this land, these figures seem incredible. It's no wonder then that the absentee landlord is a strong believer in property rights. Without them his vulnerable land might actually be used to the advantage of the user.

III. Capitalists have always been great believers in the sovereign "rights" of nations. Ayn Rand, for example, thinks it perfectly consistent with her brand of freedom that the United States government should tax the people within its borders to support an army which costs tens of billions of dollars each year. It is true that Miss Rand opposes the war in Vietnam. But why? Because "IT DOES NOT SERVE ANY NATIONAL INTEREST OF THE UNITED STATES."[95]* So we see that our advocate of "limited government" wouldn't go so far as to limit its strongest arm: the military. Eighty billion dollars a year for national "defence" doesn't seem to phase her in the least—in fact, she would like to add on a few billion more to make "an army career comparable to the standards of the civilian labour market."[96]

As every anarchist knows, a frontier is nothing more than an imaginary line drawn by a group of men with vested interests on their side of the line. That "nations" should exist is an absurdity. That a highwayman (in the uniform of a customs official) should rob people as they cross these imaginary lines and turn back others who haven't the proper pieces of paper is an obscenity too indecent to relate here—there may be children reading. But if there are children reading, perhaps they can enlighten their elders about the obvious—as they did when the emperor went out in his "new" clothes. The nationalists of the world are strutting about without a stitch of reason on. Can only a child see this?

IV. The cruelest "right"—and the one least understood today—is the exclusive right of governments to issue money. There was a time about a hundred years ago when nearly everyone was aware of the currency question. For several decades in the United States it was THE political issue. Whole political parties formed around it (e.g. the Greenback and Populist parties). William Jennings Bryan, the three-time Democratic candidate for the presidency, rose to fame with his "easy money" speeches; next to Lincoln's Gettysburg address, his "cross of gold" speech is probably the best-known

---

*   Her emphasis.

public oration of 19th century America. Yet today virtually everyone accepts the currency question as settled. Governments issue the money people use and they never give it a second thought—it's just there, like the sun and the moon. The capitalist is vitally interested in the government's exclusive right to issue money. The capitalist is, by definition, the holder of capital; and the government, by making only a certain type of capital (namely gold) the legal basis of all money, gives to the capitalist a monopoly power to compel all holders of property other than the kind thus privileged, as well as all non-proprietors, to pay tribute to the capitalist for the use of a circulating medium and instrument of credit which is absolutely necessary to carry out commerce and reap the benefits of the division of labour. A crude example of how this system works is given by the Angolan "native tax." The Portuguese whites in Angola found it difficult to get black labour for their coffee plantations, so they struck upon a rather ingenious scheme: tax the natives and the natives, having to pay their tax in MONEY, would be forced to sell their labour to the only people who could give it to them—the whiteman.[97]

The same thing goes on today on a more sophisticated level in our more "civilised" societies. The worker needs money to carry out the business of everyday life. He needs food, he needs housing, he needs clothing. To get these things he needs MONEY. And to get money he has to sell the only thing he's got: his labour. Since he MUST sell his labour, he is put into a very bad bargaining position with the buyers of labour: the capitalists. This is how the capitalist grows rich. He buys labour in a cheap market and sells his products back to the worker in a dear one. This is what Marx called the "surplus value theory" of labour. His analysis (at least here) was right; his solution to the problem was wrong.

The way Marx saw out of this trap was to abolish money. The worker would then get the equivalent of his labour by pooling his products with other workers and taking out what he needed. I've already exposed the weak points of this theory. What is the individualist alternative?

MUTUALISM: THE ECONOMICS OF FREEDOM

"There is perhaps no business which yields a profit so certain and liberal as the business of banking and exchange, and it is proper that it should be open as far as practicable to the most free competition and its advantages shared by all classes of people."
—CHIEF JUSTICE ROGER B. TANEY, 1837

When it comes to economics, most anarchists reveal an ignorance verging on the indecent. For example, in the first piece of the first issue of the new *Anarchy* the California Libertarian Alliance talks in all seriousness of "Marx's 'labour theory of value,' which causes communist governments to repress homosexuals."[98] Now, passing over the fact that Adam Smith developed the principles of this theory long before Marx was even born, I can't for the life of me see what the labour theory of value has to do with the repression of homosexuals—be they communist, capitalist, or mercantilist. Kropotkin was no better; in his "Conquest of Bread" he shows a total lack of any economic sense, as he amply demonstrates by his rejection of the very foundation of any rational economic system: the division of labour. "A society that will satisfy the needs of all, and which will know how to organise production, will also have to make a clean sweep of several prejudices concerning industry, and first of all of the theory often preached by economists—The Division of Labour Theory—which we are going to discuss in the next chapter....It is this horrible principle, so noxious to society, so brutalising to the individual, source of so much harm, that we propose to discuss in its divers manifestations."[99] He then fills the next two pages of perhaps the shortest chapter in history with a discussion of this theory "in its divers manifestations." In these few paragraphs he fancies himself as having overturned the economic thought of centuries and to have struck "a crushing blow at the theory of the division of labour which was supposed to be so sound."[100] Let's see just how sound it is.

Primitive man discovered two great advantages to social life. The first was man's ability to gain knowledge, not only through personal experience, but also through the experience of others. By learning from others, man was able to acquire knowledge which he could never have gained alone.

This knowledge was handed down from generation to generation—growing with each passing year, until today every individual has at his fingertips a wealth of information which took thousands of years to acquire. The second great advantage of social life was man's discovery of trade. By being able to exchange goods, man discovered that he was able to concentrate his efforts on a particular task at which he was especially good and/or which he especially liked. He could then trade the products of his labour for the products of the labour of others who specialised in other fields. This was found to be mutually beneficial to all concerned.

That the division of labour is beneficial when A produces one thing better than B and when B produces another thing better than A was obvious even to the caveman. Each produces that which he does best and trades with the other to their mutual advantage. But what happens when A produces BOTH things better than B? David Ricardo answered this question when he expounded his law of association over 150 years ago. This law is best illustrated by a concrete example. Let us say that Jones can produce one pair of shoes in 3 hours compared to Smith's 5 hours. Also let us say that Jones can produce one bushel of wheat in 2 hours compared to Smith's 4 hours (cf. *Table I*). If each man is to work 120 hours, what is the most advantageous way of dividing up the work? *Table II* shows three cases: the two extremes where one man does only one job while the other man does the other, and the middle road where each man divides his time equally between jobs. It is clear from *Table III* that it is to the advantage of BOTH men that the most productive man should devote

Table I: Productivity Rates

	Time Necessary to Produce One Pair of Shoes (Hours)	Time Necessary to Produce One Bushel of Wheat (Hours)
Jones	3	2
Smith	5	4

Table II: Productivity Under Division of Labor

		Hours of Shoemaking	Hours of Farming	Shoes Produced	Bushels of Wheat
	Jones	120	0	40	0
Case 1	Smith	0	120	0	30
	Total	120	120	40	30
	Jones	60	60	20	30
Case 2	Smith	60	60	12	15
	Total	120	120	32	45
	Jones	0	120	0	60
Case 3	Smith	120	0	24	0
	Total	120	120	24	60

Table III: Time Necessary to Produce the Same Amount of Goods While Working Alone (Hours)

	Jones	Smith
Case 1	120 + 60 = 180	200 + 120 = 320
Case 2	96 + 90 = 186	160 + 180 = 340
Case 3	72 + 120 = 192	120 + 240 = 360

ALL of his energies to the job which he does best (relative to the other) while the least productive man concentrates his energies on the other job (CASE 3). It is interesting to note that in the reverse situation (CASE 1)—which is also the least productive case—the drop in productivity is only 6% for Jones (the best worker), while for Smith it's a whopping 11%. So the division of labour, while helping both men, tends to help the least productive worker more than his more efficient workmate—a fact which opponents of this idea should note well.

These figures show something which is pretty obvious intuitively. A skilled surgeon, after many years invested in schooling, internship, practice, etc., may find his time more productively spent in actually performing operations than in washing his surgical instruments in preparation for these operations. It would seem natural, then, for him to hire a medical student (say for 1 pound per hour) to do the washing up job while he does the operating (for say 3 pounds per hour). Even if the surgeon could wash his own instruments twice as fast as the student, this division of labour would be profitable for all concerned.

If the earth were a homogeneous sphere, equally endowed with natural resources at each and every point of its surface, and if each man were equally capable of performing every task as well as his neighbour, then the division of labour would have no ECONOMIC meaning. There would be no material advantage to letting someone else do for you what you could do equally well yourself. But the division of labour would have arisen just the same because of the variety of human tastes. It is a fact of human nature that not all people like doing the same things. Kropotkin may think this unfortunate, but I'm afraid that's the way human beings are built. And as long as this is the case, people are going to WANT to specialise their labour and trade their products with one another.

Given the advantages of the division of labour, what is to be the method by which man exchanges his products? Primitive man devised the barter system for this purpose. But it wasn't long before the limitations of this system became apparent:

"Let Peter own a horse; let James own a cow and a pig; let James's cow and pig, taken together, be worth precisely as much as Peter's horse; let Peter and James desire to make an exchange; now, what shall prevent them from making the exchange by direct barter? Again, let Peter own the horse; let

James own the cow; and let John own the pig. Peter cannot exchange his horse for the cow, because he would lose by the transaction; neither—and for the same reason—can he exchange it for the pig. The division of the horse would result in the destruction of its value. The hide, it is true, possesses an intrinsic value; and a dead horse makes excellent manure for a grapevine; nevertheless, the division of a horse results in the destruction of its value as a living animal. But if Peter barters his horse with Paul for an equivalent in wheat, what shall prevent him from so dividing his wheat as to qualify himself to offer to James an equivalent for his cow and to John an equivalent for his pig? If Peter trades thus with James and John the transaction is still barter, though the wheat serves as currency and obviates the difficulty in making change."[101]

Thus currency (i.e, money) was born. Many things have served as money throughout the ages: slaves, gunpowder, and even human skulls, to name but a few. The New Hebrides used feathers for their money and in Ethiopia salt circulated as the currency for centuries. But by far the most popular medium of exchange became the precious metals, gold and silver. There were several reasons for this: (1) Unlike feathers or skulls, they have intrinsic value as metals. (2) They are sufficiently rare as to impose difficulty in producing them and sufficiently common as to make it not impossible to do so. (3) Their value fluctuates relatively little with the passing of time. Even large strikes—such as those in California and Alaska—failed to devalue gold to any appreciable extent. (4) They are particularly sturdy commodities, loosing relatively little due to the wear and tear of circulation. (5) They are easily divisible into fractional parts to facilitate small purchases. For these and other reasons, gold and silver became universally recognised as standards of value. Certain quantities of these metals became the units by which man measured the worth of an object. For example, the pound sterling, lira, and ruble were originally terms for metallic weight while the drachma means literally a handful.

As long as these metals served purely as just another commodity to be bartered—albeit a very useful commodity—there was no inherent advantage in possessing these metals as such. It was not until governments declared them the sole LEGAL medium of exchange that gold and silver became intrinsically oppressive. Governments, by monetising gold and silver automatically demonetised every other item of capital.* It is this monopoly which has been the chief obstacle in preventing men from obtaining the product of their labour and which permitted the few men who controlled the money supply to roll up such large fortunes at the expense of labour.

As long as the monetary structure was directly tied to gold and silver, the volume of money was limited by the amount of gold and silver available for coinage. It is for this reason that paper money—backed by "hard money"—came into being. The paper money was simply a promise "to pay the bearer on demand" its equivalent in specie (i.e. gold or silver). Hence the words "note" and "bill," which imply debt. Governments were at first reluctant to issue paper money. But the scarcity of money in an increasingly commercial world soon forced them to recant. The men of wealth, well aware of the threat that "easy money" posed to their "hard money," insisted that such money be based solely on the wealth they already possessed. Governments readily fell into line. In the United States, from 1866, anyone issuing circulating notes was slapped with a tax of 10% until it was completely outlawed in 1936. The British government was even more severe; it gave the Bank of England monopoly rights to issue "bank notes" as early as 1844.[102]

When a man is forced to barter his products for money, in order to have money to barter for such other products that he might want, he is put at a disadvantage which the capital-

---

* A natural question arises here: "That may have been true up until 40 years ago, but haven't governments since abandoned the gold standard?" The answer is no. As long as the United States government promises to buy and sell gold at $35 an ounce and as long as the International Monetary Fund (which stabilises the exchange rates) is based on gold and U.S. dollars, the world remains on the gold standard.

ist is all too ready to exploit. William B. Greene was one of the first to observe this fact:

> "Society established gold and silver as a circulating medium, in order that exchanges of commodities might be FACILITATED; but society made a mistake in so doing; for by this very act it gave to a certain class of men the power of saying what exchanges shall, and what exchanges shall not, be FACILITATED by means of this very circulating medium. The monopolisers of the precious metals have an undue power over the community; they can say whether money shall, or shall not, be permitted to exercise its legitimate functions. These men have a VETO on the action of money, and therefore on exchanges of commodity; and they will not take off their VETO until they have received usury, or, as it is more politely termed, interest on their money. Here is the great objection to the present currency. Behold the manner in which the absurdity inherent in a specie currency—or, what is still worse, in a currency of paper based upon specie—manifests itself in actual operation! The mediating value which society hoped would facilitate exchanges becomes an absolute marketable commodity, itself transcending all reach of mediation. The great natural difficulty which originally stood in the way of exchanges is now the private property of a class, and this class cultivates this difficulty, and make money out of it, even as a farmer cultivates his farm and makes money by his labour. But there is a difference between the farmer and the usurer; for the farmer benefits the community as well as himself, while every dollar made by the usurer is a dollar taken from the pocket of some other individual, since the usurer cultivates nothing but an actual obstruction."[103]

The legitimate purpose of money is to facilitate exchange. As Greene shows, specie—or money based on specie—accomplishes this purpose, but only at a terrible price to the user. The solution to the problem is to devise a money which has no value as a COMMODITY, only as a circulating medium. This money should also be available in such quantity as not to hamper any exchanges which may be desired. The organ for creating such a currency Greene called a "mutual bank."*

Before considering the operations of a mutual bank, I'd like to look at how an ordinary bank functions. Let us say that Mr Brown, who owns a farm worth a few thousand pounds, needs 500 pounds to buy seed and equipment for the coming year. Not having that kind of money on hand, he goes to the bank to borrow it. The bank readily agrees—on the condition that at the end of the year Brown not only pays back the 500 pounds borrowed, but also 50 pounds which they call "interest." Farmer Brown has no choice; he needs MONEY because that is all the seed dealer will accept as "legal tender." So he agrees to the conditions set down by the bank. After a year of hard work, and with a bit of luck from the weather, he harvests his crops and exchanges (i.e. "sells") his produce—for money. He takes 550 pounds to the bank and cancels his debt. The net result of all this is that some banker is 50 pounds richer for doing a minimal amount of work (perhaps a few hours of bookkeeping) at no risk to himself (the farm was collateral), while Mr Brown is 50 pounds out of pocket.

Now let's see where Greene's idea leads us. A group of people get together and decide to set up a mutual bank. The bank will issue notes which all members of the bank agree to accept as "money." Taking the above example, Mr Brown could get five hundred of these notes by mortgaging his farm and discounting with the bank a mortgage note for that sum. With the notes, he buys his seed from Smith and some tools from Jones. Smith and Jones in turn exchange some of these

---

*   Proudhon's bank, "la banque du peuple," is essentially the same. For a detailed account of the workings of each bank see Greene's *Mutual Banking* and Proudhon's *Solution of the Social Problem* and *Revolution in the Nineteenth Century*.

newly acquired notes for some things they need. And so on until the end of the year when Brown exchanges his farm produce and receives for them—mutual bank notes. Does all this sound familiar? It should, for up until now, from all outward appearances, there has been no difference between our mutual bank and an ordinary specie bank. But it's here, however, that the change comes in. Mr Brown goes to the mutual bank with his notes and gives the bank 500 of them plus ONE OR TWO extra to help pay for the operating expenses of the bank over the past year. The bank cancels his mortgage and Mr Brown walks away thinking how nice it is to be a member of such a wonderful bank.

Now notice that it was never mentioned that Smith and Jones were members of the bank. They may have been, but it wasn't necessary. Smith, the seed dealer, might not belong to the bank and yet be willing to accept its notes. He's in business, after all, and if the only money Brown has is mutual money, that's all right with him—as long as he can get rid of it when HE wants to buy something. And of course he can because he knows there are other members of the bank pledged to receiving these notes. Besides, Brown will need at least 500 of them eventually to pay off his mortgage. So Smith accepts the money, and he too profits from this novel scheme. In fact, the only one who seems to be any the worse is the poor usurous banker. But I'm afraid he will just have to find himself an honest job and work for his living like everyone else.

John Stuart Mill defined capital as "wealth appropriated to reproductive employment." In our example above, farmer Brown's 500 pounds is capital since he intends to use it for creating new wealth. But Mr Brown can use his capital in any number of ways: he may decide to use it to buy seeds for planting corn; or he may decide that his ground is better suited for growing wheat, or he may decide to invest in a new tractor. This 500 pounds, then, is liquid capital or, as Greene called it, disengaged capital. When Mr Brown buys his seeds and tools, these things are still designed for "reproductive employment," and are therefore still capital. But what kind of capital? Evidently, frozen or engaged capital. He then plants his seeds and harvests his crops with the aid of his new tractor. The produce he grows is no longer capital because it is no longer capable of being "appropriated to reproductive employment." What is it, then? Evidently, it is product. Mr Brown then takes his goods to town and sells them at market value for somewhat more than the 500 pounds he originally started out with. This "profit" is entirely due to his labour as a farmer (and perhaps to some extent his skill as a salesman). The money he receives for his goods become, once again, liquid capital. So we have came full circle: liquid capital becomes frozen capital; frozen capital becomes product; product becomes liquid capital. And the cycle starts all over again.

A society is prosperous when money flows freely—that is when each man is able to easily convert his product into liquid capital. A society is unprosperous when money is tight—that is, when exchange is difficult to effect. Mutual banking makes as much money available as is necessary. When a man needs money he simply goes to his friendly mutual bank, mortgages some property, and receives the notes of the bank in return. What this system does is to allow a man to circulate his CREDIT. Whoever goes to a mutual bank and mortgages some of his property will always receive money, for a mutual bank can issue money to any extent. This money will always be good because it is all based on actual property which, if necessary, could be sold to pay off bad debts. The mutual bank, of course, would never give PERSONAL credit, for to do so would give the notes an element of risk and render them unstable. But what about the man with no property to pledge? Greene answered this question as follows:

> "If we knew of a plan whereby, through an act of the legislature, every member of the community might be made rich, we would destroy this petition and draw up another embodying that plan. Meanwhile, we affirm that no system was ever devised so beneficial to the poor as the sys-

tem of mutual banking; for if a man having nothing to offer in pledge, has a friend who is a property holder and that friend is willing to furnish security for him, he can borrow money at the mutual bank at a rate of 1% interest a year; whereas, if he should borrow at the existing banks, he would be obliged to pay 6%. Again as mutual banking will make money exceedingly plenty, it will cause a rise in the rate of wages, thus benefiting the man who has no property but his bodily strength; and it will not cause a proportionate increase in the price of the necessaries of life: for the price of provisions, etc., depends on supply and demand; and mutual banking operates, not directly on supply and demand, but to the diminution of the rate of interest on the medium of exchange. But certain mechanics and farmers say, 'We borrow no money, and therefore pay no interest. How, then does this thing concern us?' Harken, my friends! let us reason together. I have an impression on my mind that it is precisely the class who have no dealings with the banks, and derive no advantages from them, that ultimately pay all the interest money that is paid. When a manufacturer borrows money to carry on his business, he counts the interest he pays as a part of his expenses, and therefore adds the amount of interest to the price of his goods. The consumer who buys the goods pays the interest when he pays for the goods; and who is the consumer, if not the mechanic and the farmer? If a manufacturer could borrow money at 1%, he could afford to undersell all his competitors, to the manifest advantage of the farmer and mechanic. The manufacturer would neither gain nor lose; the farmer and mechanic, who have no dealings with the bank, would gain the whole difference; and the bank—which, were it not for the competition of the mutual bank, would have loaned the money at 6% interest—would lose the whole difference. It is the indirect relation of the bank to the farmer and mechanic, and not its direct relation to the manufacturer and merchant, that enables it to make money."[104]

Mutual banking, by broadening the currency base, makes money plentiful. The resulting stimulus to business would create an unprecedented demand for labour—a demand which would always be in excess of the supply. Then, as Benjamin Tucker observed:

"When two labourers are after one employer, wages fall, but when two employers are after one labourer, wages rise. Labour will then be in a position to dictate its wages, and will thus secure its natural wage, its entire product. Thus the same blow that strikes interest down will send wages up. But this is not all. Down will go profits also. For merchants, instead of buying at high prices on credit, will borrow money of the banks at less than one percent, buy at low prices for cash, and correspondingly reduce the prices of their goods to their customers. And with the rest will go house-rent. For no one who can borrow capital at one percent with which to build a house of his own will consent to pay rent to a landlord at a higher rate than that."[105]

Unlike the "boom and bust" cycles we now experience under the present system, mutualism would know nothing but "boom." For the present "busts" come when the economy is "overheated" and when there is so-called "overproduction." As long as most of humanity lead lives of abject poverty, we can never speak realistically of "over-production." And as long as each hungry belly comes with a pair of hands, mutualism will be there to give those hands work to fill that belly.

AN AFTERWORD TO COMMUNIST-ANARCHIST READERS

What generally distinguishes you from your communist brother in some authoritarian sect is your basic lack of dogmatism. The state socialist is always towing some party line. When it comes to creative thinking his brain is in a mental straitjacket, with no more give and take in his mind than you will find in the mind of a dog watching a rabbit hole. You, on the contrary, pride yourself on being "your own man." Having no leaders, prophets, Messiahs, or Popes to refer to for divine guidance, you can afford to use YOUR mind to analyse the facts as YOU see them and come up with YOUR conclusions. You are, in your fundamental metaphysics, an agnostic. You are broad minded to a fault...how else could you have read this far?

But when it comes to economics, your mind suddenly becomes rigid. You forget your sound anarchist principles and surrender without a struggle the one thing that makes you an anarchist: your freedom. You suddenly develop an enormous capacity for believing and especially for believing what is palpably not true. By invoking a set of second hand dogmas (Marxist hand-me-downs) which condemn outright the free market economy, you smuggle in through the back door authoritarian ideas which you had barred from the main entrance. In commendably searching for remedies against poverty, inequality and injustice, you forsake the doctrine of freedom for the doctrine of authority and in so doing come step by step to endorse all the fallacies of Marxist economics. A few years ago S. E. Parker wrote an open letter to the editors of *Freedom* in which he said:

"The trouble is that what you call 'anarchism' is at best merely a hodge-podge, halfway position precariously suspended between socialism and anarchism. You yearn for the ego-sovereignty, the liberating individualism, that is the essence of anarchism, but remain captives of the democratic-proletarian-collectivist myths of socialism. Until you can cut the umbilical cord that still connects you to the socialist womb you will never be able to come to your full power as self-owning individuals. You will still be lured along the path to the lemonade springs and cigarette trees of the Big Rock Candy Mountains." [106]

This article was written for you in hopes of relieving you of your schizophrenic condition. The fact that you call yourself an anarchist shows that you have an instinctual "feeling" for freedom. I hope that this article will encourage you to seek to put that feeling on a sound foundation. I am confident that when you do, you will reject your communist half.

REFERENCES

1. Joseph Stalin, *Anarchism or Socialism* (Moscow; Foreign Languages Publishing House, 1950), p. 85. Written in 1906 but never finished.

2. Ibid., pp. 90-1.

3. Ibid., p.95.

4. Ibid., p. 87.

5. Pierre-Joseph Proudhon, *What is Property: An Inquiry into the Principle of Right and of Government*, trans. Benjamin R. Tucker (London: William Reeves), p. 260. Originally published in French in 1840.

6. Bill Dwyer, "This World", "Freedom," March 27, 1971.

7. Pierre Kropotkine, *Paroles d'un Revolté* (Paris: Ernest Flammarion, 1885), pp. 318-9.

8. Paul Eltzbacher, *Anarchism: Exponents of the Anarchist Philosophy*, trans. Steven T. Byington, ed. James J. Martin (London: Freedom Press, 1960), p. 108. *Der Anarchismus* was originally published in Berlin in 1900.

9. Ibid., p. 109.

10. Ibid., p. 110.

11. Herbert Spencer, "*The Man Versus The State*," ed. Donald MacRae (London: Penguin Books, 1969), p. 151. Originally published in 1884.

12. Prince Peter Kropotkin, *The Conquest of Bread* (London: Chapman & Hall, Ltd., 1906), p. 41.

13. Eltzbacher, op. cit., p. 101.

14. Kropotkin, op. cit., p. 209.

15. Ibid., p. 206.

16. Henry David Thoreau, "Journal," March 11, 1856.

17. Kropotkin, op. cit., p. 206.

18. Ibid., p. 205.

19. Errico Malatesta, *Anarchy* (London: Freedom Press, 1949), p. 33.

Originally published in 1907.

20. Alexander Berkman, *A.B.C. of Anarchism* (London: Freedom Press, 1964), p. 27. This is the abbreviated version of the Vanguard Press *ABC of Communist Anarchism* which appeared in 1929.

21. Ibid., p. 28.

22. Ibid., p. 29.

23. Ibid., p. 25.

24. "Italy: An Illness of Convenience," *Newsweek*, January 4, 1971, p. 44.

25. "Un Forum Législatif de la Classe Ouvrière?", *Granma* (French edition), January 31, 1971, p. 3.

26. "Cuba Announces Labor Penalties For Loafers," *The International Herald Tribune,* March 19, 1971, p. 4.

27. Theodore Roszak, *The Making of a Counter Culture* (Garden City, New York: Anchor Books, 1969), p. 29.

28. Kropotkin, op. cit., pp. 236-7.

29. Mikhail Bakunin, *The Political Philosophy of Bakunin: Scientific Anarchism*, ed. G. P. Maximoff (New York: The Free Press, 1953), p. 285.

30. Homer Lane, *Talks to Parents and Teachers* (London: George Allen & Unwin, Ltd., 1928), p. 121.

31. Paul Goodman, *Compulsory Mis-education* and *The Community of Scholars* (New York: Vintage Books, 1962, 1964), p. 174.

32. Erich Fromm, *Fear of Freedom* (London: Routledge & Kegan Paul, Ltd., 1960), p. 34. First published in the United States in 1942 under the title *Escape from Freedom*.

33. Petr Kropotkin, *Mutual Aid: A Factor of Evolution* (Boston: Extending Horizons Books, 1955), p. 297. This book first appeared in London in 1902.

34. Ibid., p. 166.

35. Ibid., p. 169.

36. Ibid., p. 176.

37. Ibid., p. 176.

38. Ibid., pp. 172-3.

39. Ibid., p. 176.

40. Ibid., p. 174.

41. Ibid., p. 177.

REFERENCES • 77

42. Ibid., p. 194.

43. Ibid., p. 194.

44. Ibid,, p. 194.

45. Ibid., pp. 194-5.

46. Ibid., pp. 209-10.

47. Ibid., p. 214.

48. Kropotkine, *Paroles*, p. 333.

49. Kropotkin, *Mutual Aid*, p. 215.

50. Ibid., p. 217.

51. Ibid., p. 219.

52. Rudolf Rocker, *Nationalism and Culture*, trans. Ray E. Chase (Los Angeles: Rocker Publications Committee, 1937), p. 92.

53. Ibid., p. 91.

54. Ibid., p. 92.

55. Proudhon, op. cit., pp. 248-51.

56. Herbert Marcuse, *Reason and Revolution: Hegel and the Rise of Social Theory* (London: Routledge & Kegan Paul, Ltd., 1967), p. 435. This quotation was taken from the supplementary chapter written in 1954. The original book was first published by Oxford University Press in 1941.

57. Kropotkine, *Paroles*, p. 341.

58. Ibid., p. 342.

59. Noam Chomsky, "Notes on Anarchism," *Anarchy*, issue 116, October, 1970, p. 316.

60. Ibid., p. 318.

61. Bob Dylan, "Subterranean Homesick Blues," 1965.

62. Eltzbacher, op. cit., p. 89.

63. Ibid., p. 57.

64. Benjamin R. Tucker, *Instead of a Book (By a Man Too Busy to Write One)* (New York: Benj. R. Tucker, 1897), p. 401. Reprinted from *Liberty*, May 12, 1888.

65. Max Stirner (Johann Kaspar Schmidt), *The Ego and His Own: The Case of the Individual Against Authority,* trans. Steven T. Byington (New York: Libertarian Book Club, 1963), p. 298. *Der Einzige und sein Eigentum* was written in 1844 and translated into English in

1907, when it was published in New York by Benj. Tucker.

66. Agatha Christie, *Destination Unknown* (London: Fontana Books), p. 98.

67. Spencer, op, cit., pp. 323-4.

68. Stalin, op. cit., p. 97.

69. Robert Burns, "To a Mouse," 1785, stanza 7.

70. S. E. Parker, "Letters", *Freedom*, February 27, 1971.

71. Tucker, *Instead of a Book*, p. 413. Reprinted from *Liberty*, October 4, 1884.

72. Tucker, "Instead of a Book," p. 422. Reprinted from *Liberty*, June 23, 1888.

73. Stirner, op. cit., p. 210.

74. Ibid., p. 319.

75. Proudhon, op. cit., pp. 243-4.

76. Stirner, op. cit., p. 179.

77. Ibid., p. 291.

78. "At the Summit of the Affluent U.S. Society," *The International Herald Tribune*. March 19, 1971, p. 1.

79. *Newsweek*, February 1, 1971 , p. 44.

80. Stirner, op. cit., pp. 270-2.

81. Tucker, *Instead of a Book*, p. 404. Reprinted from "Liberty," April 28, 1888.

82. Quoted from Charles A. Reich's article in *The New Yorker* magazine, "The Greening of American," September 26, 1970.

83. G. D. H. Cole, *What Everybody Wants To Know About Money* (London: Victor Gollancz Ltd., 1933), pp. 526-7.

84. Ken Knudson, "Letters", *Freedom*, November 14, 1970.

85. Ian S. Sutherland, "Doomsday & After," *Freedom*, February 27, 1971.

86. "Laissez Faire," *Encyclopaedia Britannica*, 1965, vol. XIII, p. 606.

87. Ayn Rand, *Capitalism: The Unknown Ideal* (New York: Signet Books, 1967), p 320.

88. Ibid., p. 331.

89. Ibid., p. 131.

90. Ibid., pp. 131-2.

REFERENCES   • 79

91. Ibid., pp. 132-3.

92. Ibid., p, 132.

93. Ibid., p. 134.

94. "Geographical Summaries: Area and Population," *Encyclopaedia Britannica Atlas,* 1965, p. 199.

95. Rand, op. cit., p. 224.

96. Ibid., p. 229.

97. Douglas Marchant, "Angola," *Anarchy* 112, June, 1970, p. 184.

98. "Libertarian Message to Gay Liberation," *Anarchy,* February, 1971, p. 2.

99. Kropotkin, *Conquest of Bread*, pp. 245 & 248.

100. Ibid., p. 250.

101. William B. Greene, "Mutual Banking," from Proudhon's *Solution of the Social Problem*, ed. Henry Cohen (New York: Vanguard Press, 1927), p. 177.

102. "Money," *Encyclopaedia Britannica*, 1965, vol. XV, p. 703.

103. Greene, op. cit., p. 180.

104. Ibid., pp. 196-7.

105. Tucker, *Instead of a Book* p. 12, Reprinted from "Liberty," March 10, 1888.

106. S. E. Parker, "Enemies of Society: An Open Letter to the Editors of Freedom," *Minus One*, October-December, 1967, p. 4.